MW00927715

The Paranormal Chronicles presents

Ghost sex: The Violation

By G L Davies

Introduction

If you haven't already guessed this book is based on two very controversial subjects, sex and the paranormal. I would imagine that one or both are of some interest to you but before we begin I must warn you that this book, this paranormal account, is unnerving and the graphic and descriptive nature of the spectral intrusion and violation may be both unsettling and offensive to those of a more conservative persuasion.

Are you still there? Good, then let's start with a deep and profound question that I need to ask you, to ask yourself. It is important that you do so, as you need to know what bearing, if any, sex has your life. As you will have concluded by the title of this book, sexual violation is a key theme in the investigation we are to conduct. Do not base this answer on what you have been told to believe, or one you expect others to believe is your answer. You must be honest. The question is: What does sex mean to you?

Is the physical act of sex a way of achieving closeness, possibly to solidify a bond? Is sex a way of differentiating a romantic relationship from that of a plutonic one? Maybe sex is a way of getting people to like you, so that you feel attractive and desirable? Do you give yourself as an expression of gratitude and acceptance? Perhaps to some it is a physical and emotional expression, and to some just an animalistic and carnal urge that is programmed into the human condition to simply fornicate and reproduce, a part of us as normal as breathing and excreting. Is sex the heartbeat of a relationship? Or is sex just good exercise and an enjoyable, fun and adrenaline fuelled rollercoaster of physicality and pleasure? It might be a mixture of feelings but whatever sex means to you, it is constantly there. Whether you have too much, too little, have abstained or can't get any at all, we all realise that sex is an important part of our lives. However, imagine if you will that your body is at the whim of an unknown and unseen visitor, which will conduct an illegal intrusion upon you. You cannot stop it, reason or plead with it, or even ask for help from such tangible institutions as the police, medical or psychological practices. No justice can be served on the entity that has sexual union at its own malevolent whim. Just when you feel that you can despair no longer, you have given in to the mal-treatment and to the defilement; suddenly you realize that this paranormal incursion into your life may not be as bad as you first thought. Can you envisage that you have submitted and have accepted this taboo as a personally justifiable occurrence?

How would that affect those close to you? Consider your current partner if you have one and ask yourself how would they react if you were to have a paranormal affair? Could they lie next to you at night content in the knowledge that a metaphysical visitor, with a power far superior to our own, is having carnal relations with you? That something unearthly and quixotic is pleasuring you in a way they cannot. Would they take this in their stride, or see it as some negligence on your behalf, or perhaps that of God? Could you both look at each other the same way knowing that a third member was now part of your sacred relationship? There are so many questions that you will consider once you have undertaken this read and joined me on this investigation. This is indeed a journey that perhaps you did not expect to undertake today.

The paranormal of course is based on your own subjectivity and the experiences or beliefs that you have. Some people are hardened to this subject and can take the unexplained in their stride, but for some it is a terrifying topic. Regardless of your stance, I believe this investigation will have elements that will take you by surprise, the detail and ferocity of the events bestowed upon the home will shock you.

I have investigated the paranormal for over twenty five years. I have witnessed some truly baffling sights and experiences and have been able to bring peace to troubled and disturbed people by offering a solid and rational explanation for the events happening to them. In some cases I have been given no choice but to notify the authorities as the events perceived to be occurring are due, sadly, to a breakdown of mental and emotional functionality that have the possibility to do harm to others. This case, the one before you now, is like nothing I have ever been involved with. It breaks new grounds in terms of the experiences perceived by the witness's and by the information collated in the subsequent investigation that book ends this account.

If you think you know about paranormal encounters, if you think this is just a Welsh version of the *Entity* or a more sexually descriptive version of the potter's wheel scene in *Ghost,* then I ask you to reconsider and push away any preconceptions of what you are about to read. If the accounts presented are real, then every single one of us on this blue globe, spinning in the cosmos, is susceptible to a terrifying and illegal breach onto our physicality. If your house is deemed to be haunted then maybe the events happening so far just herald far more terrifying activity yet to occur.

I am by my own admission no William Shakespeare and where I may make grammatical and spelling errors I make up with a passion and enthusiasm to uncover the truth, to report to those willing to take the time to read these accounts of paranormal events happening to real people, just like you. For those of you that read my previous offering of *A most haunted house*, which was the raw and gritty account of a haunting so devastating that it tore the world apart of a young couple just trying to settle together and find happiness in a new home, then this account is just as confounding. Not only by the spirits need for sexual intrusion, but also for the chilling and terrifying haunting that took place in the home and its effects on the other members of the household. This is not just an account of a ghost's sexual wrong doing, but of a paranormal infiltration and haunting into a normal household in a town in Pembrokeshire.

The investigation and interviews I conducted have some of the strangest and unique factors that I have transcribed. The Paranormal exceeds what is deemed physically possible based upon our times scientific assumptions so, as I did with *A most haunted house,* I ask that you take the account and digest it and fathom it in a fashion best suited to you. It is not for me to force upon you any beliefs of what occurred at this home in Pembroke Dock, but for you to use your own beliefs, theories and philosophies and decide for yourself. Unlike *A most haunted house* I was able, along with a psychologist, to spend a week at the home to conduct a more thorough investigation. After the family's account which follows shortly, my investigation shall be presented to you to help you discern on the nature of the events. You are now the investigator and through my thorough interview techniques I ask that you look for evidence and clues on what you believe is fact or fiction.

The transcripts are in the words of the people involved. Often it shall be raw, gritty and exceptionally vulgar and colourful at times but these are the ways in which the family express themselves. This is their story and I ask that you take the time to concentrate on the accounts they tell and not the way they deliver it, as through their own expression and words you get a closer and truer look at what they experienced. You get a feel on their backgrounds and their upbringings, the very fabric of their countenance. We would also like you to note that during the questions regarding the sexual and graphic nature of the offense that a female investigator accompanied myself for those sessions and that the names of the people involved have obviously been changed to protect the anonymity of the family. Dates, locations and details that could link to the family have been changed and the accounts have been arranged into a more chronological fashion so, you, the reader can become more involved in the events as they happened. The family have given me full permission to publish their story on the basis that if others out there have had similar experiences; it may help make sense of what happened. This account is shocking, chilling and exceptionally detailed in places so be warned this paranormal chronicle may not be to everyone's liking.

Are you still there?

Excellent, then let's meet the family.

Lisa

I meet with Lisa at her home in Pembroke Dock. Pembroke Dock is a town in Pembrokeshire, south-west Wales, lying north of Pembroke on the River Cleddau. Originally a small fishing village, the town was greatly expanded from 1814 onwards following the construction of a Royal Naval Dockyard. It is the third largest town in Pembrokeshire after Haverfordwest and Milford Haven. Today, much of Pembroke Dock's maritime industry has gone. The town continues to cope with high unemployment, limited public and private investment, and decaying buildings. The town briefly had resurgence in the late 1990s and early 2000s with the arrival of large superstores and the development of the Cleddau Business Park.

Lisa sees herself as fortunate as she has worked for a national company for sixteen years, now in her early forties and mother of one, Lisa sits in her living room smoking a cigarette. She is pleasant and agreeable and her face does not reflect the trouble past she has endured. She is happy to reminisce about her childhood days and relationship with her family;

Lisa: I was born in Cambridgeshire in January 1972. It was snowing very heavily according to my Mum, and she said Dad never saw me being born, he didn't see much of us all to be honest. My old man was In the R.A.F (Royal Air force) and we travelled around a bit. We lived in Cardiff for a few years before settling in Pembrokeshire around 1980. He was posted to R.A.F Brawdy and I have been here ever since. Mum and Dad separated in 1982 and we haven't really seen him since, he left the R.A.F and became an overseas contractor for a big company. I have heard that he re-married and had a new family. I don't mind them turning up one day if they are rich, but if not they can bugger off! Most people that know me down here don't know that I am a twin, we were two girls and her name was Rose and she died when we were eight. She was run over outside a school. Dad was never the same and Mum became mixed up with some spiritualist people, I guess she was trying to hold onto to something, you know? Like maybe she wasn't gone, gone but living in heaven or as a spirit. Mum changed her outlook completely and became really spiritual and holistic. She and Dad never really were the same together. He would drink and work and she would dabble in séances and Ouija boards and things with these other women. She is convinced that Rose has had long chats with her. I never heard or seen Rose after. She was killed and it is what it is.

I liked Rose, we got on really well. You asked me earlier about whether anything like this has happened before; you asked if when I was younger I had experienced any paranormal activity. When we were about 5 or 6, Rose and I shared a room and our beds were a few feet apart. We would go to bed and we would wake up and something would land on my bed and then land on Roses, like something was jumping from bed to bed. You could not see anything, but at that age we used to find it funny. We used to call it the naughty boy as it would tickle our feet sometimes and hide things in our room. Mum shouted at us one night, as she said we were messing about and jumping around, and we were in hysterics as we were in bed laughing and it was naughty boy doing it. Mum was furious and used to threaten to take our toys away and we would be sad and say it wasn't us. She believes me now, but back then being a Mum on your own, pretty much raising two girls because Dad is working, must have been difficult and tiring. Any mother out there knows that tiredness. Mum believes now though, she believes in everything. If the Yeti and a spaceman were sat in the garden having a tea she would take it all in her stride. That's how much Rose's death affected her. It changed her beliefs so much.

I often think about naughty boy and how so many children have imaginary friends. Did Rose and I imagine him or was he really a ghost? I heard a customer talking to another lady last week, she was saying that her little boy has an imaginary friend and I smiled inside and thought, is it imaginary? Or do kids see spirits at a younger age?

After Rose was killed I was upstairs in my room, just looking at the pale grey sky, there were lots of people downstairs. I think they kept me out of the way as mum and dad were so distraught. I just looked out of the window and I felt so cold and tired. I felt like I could just sleep and never wake up again. There is a strong connection with twins, unless you are one you can never fully understand, but her pain and loss I could feel. It was almost like an echo of her passing was hitting me in a wave, slowly getting smaller and smaller until finally I knew she was gone completely. I felt like I was slipping away from this world. Then I heard a weeping, a soft sob in the room, I looked and there was nothing. I felt a hand touch my hair and a chill went through me, like a cold draught touched my bones and the crying stopped. Most people might say it was Rose, I don't think so; I think it was naughty boy, I think he was sad and he missed her. Naughty boy never did anything again, never bounced on the bed, never tickled my feet. He simply vanished. I lost two friends that day and my parents were never the same again. It is mad how in one day, one hour, and one minute, your whole life can change.

Mum had an interesting theory that the reason naughty boy was sad was because he was leaving me behind to be with Rose. Rose would be all alone in the spirit world and I would be O.K as I had Mum and Dad and I would have a life and friends. He went to be with her and play with her and keep her company. I like that idea, naughty boy and rose forever young and playing in a place where there is no time and no illness or pain. I like that.

Dad left and Mum got a council house here in the Dock. Mum didn't seem that upset, it was like she expected it and she got even more spiritual and hippy like. She had a string of boyfriends, none lasted, and none really bothered with me, which suited me fine. I began to settle into Pembrokeshire life, I made friends, did O.K. at school and not much really happened. When I was sixteen I met this guy called Ian, who lived at a farm not far from Pembroke Dock, we got on well and we went out with each other. A few months after meeting him I got pregnant and left school.

We were far too young to have children. Ian worked on his parent's farm and they paid him a pittance. They were so fucking tight, like misers. They didn't help the baby at all. It was like they were ashamed of us. Ian would pop over and he tried to be a Dad, you got to remember he was only a bit older than me; he went from hanging around with his mates and having fun to changing nappies with me in my mum's house. Mum was great, she raised Tyler like he was her own, she didn't have much but mum made sure we didn't do without. When Ian got up and left and never contacted us again, it was mum that was there, no one else, just mum. Ian's miserable twat parents never told me where he was, never helped Tyler, and never even sent us a Christmas card. I have no idea where Ian is now, I don't hate him as at times I wished I could just run away but you can't, not when you have a little baby to take care of. He could and he did. Wherever he is I hope he is ok. His parents come into the shop where I work and go out of their way to avoid me, the horrible twats. They have a grandson in his twenties and they have never met him. Tyler tries, he's a good lad and he will get there eventually, he just hasn't found out who he is yet. The sad part is that Tyler had to come back home and live with me again and what's been happening hasn't just centred on me, no, it takes it out on him as well. As a mother I feel so useless, I should be able to protect my son.

Tyler

Tyler sits before me with a roll up cigarette and a coffee. He has his mother's green eyes and brown hair. He is short and stocky and looks tired and has not shaved in several days. He is far more reserved than his mother and has a nervousness about him. He clearly is not comfortable and appears anxious about the interview process and the subject of the haunting at his home. I have to work hard, guaranteeing his anonymity, his body language shows tell-tale signs that he does not welcome another unwanted stranger into his home. He gets up and leaves and he and his mother have a hushed discussion in the kitchen. He returns, grumpily sits back down and makes a new smoke. He looks at me direct in the eye and asks again to confirm that they shall remain anonymous and that my role here is to help document the events and possibly offer a rational explanation, maybe help others experiencing the same things. I assure him, I explain what I do and how I will try and help him and his mother, he relaxes and after some small talk he begins his interview.

Tyler: You know I'm not sure about all of this, all of this ghost shit. Sometimes I think it's us, that we see things, the human race that is, like a psychological disorder, a mental illness we have that makes us believe we see ghosts and aliens and supernatural things. Maybe we developed it because we are scared of dying but we are just like ants in a nest. This world is the nest and we crawl all over it, working, screwing...dying. I think sometimes life is nothing more than that.

I'm twenty four now and I've been back living with mum for about two years. I had my own place in town when I was working at the call centre but when I lost that job after a few months I had to move back as I could not afford the rent anymore. I liked the job, they were really good to me, really supportive but I kept not turning up or coming in late. I'd have a heavy weekend and I'd be fucked on the Monday. Nice place, nice people, but not for me. It was my own fault I lost the job.

I've had a few jobs, I worked filling shelves in a supermarket in Haverfordwest but there weren't enough hours there so I quit and worked at a local tourist attraction for a summer and that was O.K but the role ended in October. I liked that job, it was good to be outside and I met some really nice people there, some nice girls.

I think if I could choose my perfect job then it would be in the army or navy or something. My granddad was a pilot or something and he got to travel the world. I have asthma and that holds me back, I should give up smoking and maybe start a health kick, a detox, but I never find the time to get around to it. I'll try in the New Year. Believe it or not I did alright in school, I got some A levels in English and geography, but I only stayed on in school as I didn't know what else to do and I didn't fancy just getting a job for the sake of it back then. I wish I hadn't done useless A-levels, I should have gone to Pembrokeshire College and got a trade like a plumber or mechanic. That's where the money is. Now I don't mind what I do as long as I get money as you don't get much on the dole, seventy odd quid a fortnight. You get treated so badly when you don't have a job, it's like you are judged, I ask the job centre people all the time for solutions and they send me on stupid courses. One course taught me how to turn on a computer, what a waste of fucking time. Mums good though, she don't ask for keep and she works full time and she lends me a bit for going out or bus fare. She's good like that. She'll come home from a day's work and make me dinner and do my washing. One day I'll look after her and make sure she's O.K and does not have to work anymore. I'd like to get her a cottage by the sea, down Broad Haven way. One day I will.

I've had a few girlfriends, last one I was with for two years but she got a job in a hotel in Portsmouth and we tried the long distance thing but it didn't really work, it was so expensive to travel down to see her and she came back about once a month and then she met someone up there, some French guy and that was that. I have some good mates here and we go to the pubs a lot and I like to play Call of Duty on my games console. I hope to get into the army; I think I would be good at that. There were adverts on T.V and I thought that could be good, I could learn a trade and see the world, meet girls, get into shape but Mum is worried about places like Afghanistan and Iraq and places like that. I tell her I wouldn't be sent there but she won't listen and she worries. One of her friend's sons was killed in Afghanistan by an Afghanistan policeman who was supposed to be on our side, as her only son I don't think she can bear to think about me out in a place like that. She is very protective.

When I was about four or five, Mum got us a council house just off town; Dad had done a runner when I was just a baby so it was just us two. Nan was about a lot too, I get on really well with Nan, she is mad as a box of snakes but a kind woman. She loves all of this haunting stuff, she tells us not to worry but she's not the one that has to live with it all the time.

I remember this one time when I was about ten and something weird had happened in the night and Mum was really freaked out. Something had happened, I'm not entirely sure; it might have been the first time the ghost had touched her. Mum is crying on the phone to Nan and Nan comes over and she's so relaxed about it saying that we had a spirit and that it was trying to communicate and show that it meant no harm and Mum was screaming that it had touched her. Nan lit some incense and blessed the house with prayers and chanting, she often does that, she blesses houses all the time, she blessed one in Haverfordwest a few years back and the people were livid with her saying she had made it worse not better. That's Nan though, barking mad.

When I was growing up in the house I can't remember really anything happening till then. I remember once lying in bed watching T.V. My bedroom door was open and I could smell a really bad smell, like shit. I thought Jeeze, the toilet is blocked or something. It was an overpowering sickly shitty smell and I sat up in my bed and there at the top of the stairs on the landing I swore I saw a man's head, like he was lying on the top of the stairs so just his head was peeping over the top step and it startled me and I let out a yelp and he vanished and the smell vanished in a blink of an eye. I remember that day really vividly the man's head looked all dirty, like it was covered in soot, like a chimney sweep and his hair was matted over his eyes and forehead and he looked to have a big black beard covered in like a grease or liquid and then it just went. He looked and smelt like a man that lived in a sewer. I was nervous to go down stairs and I stood in my bedroom door and I must have shouted for mum a million times and she came up the stairs to see if I was O.K and she asked what was wrong and I told her and she just gave me a hug and said it was O.K and that it was just her and I in the house and my mind was probably playing tricks on me. Looking back she wasn't that convincing. I told an ex-girlfriend about it once and she said it could have been a dog or a pet apart from we didn't have any pets, we never have.

When I told Nan she didn't like that story, she said to ignore it and that it wouldn't come back and not to tell Mum and that sometimes there were nasty spirits that looked and smelled awful and they were there to frightened us and make us weak so they could play tricks on us and make us sad and depressed. I wonder what Nan thought it was?

Nothing really happened for years as far as I know, not until when I was about sixteen and that was a truly awful, night. I still wake up now in the middle of the night thinking about it and it scares me so much. I'm not afraid to admit that.

Beginnings

Lisa: Tyler told you about the man at the top of the stairs? I never told him about this as he believes that it all began when he was about sixteen even though strange things had been happening in between. I always tried to hide as much as I could from him. There were things that I tried really hard to dismiss or explain to him but we will get to that later. I had to protect him from what was happening. A ten year old will not be able to comprehend all this and it could mess his head up for life, I'm surprised he is as normal as he is after everything we have been through.

When Tyler was about eight, I got a job at the place where I work now, I was so thrilled as it was not far from where we lived at the time and the hours were good in that I could drop Tyler off in at school, work and pick him up at three and on the odd nights that I needed to work late then Mum would pick him up and they would have tea and Tyler loves his Nan and she loves him so it would be good for them both. It was good to be independent again, don't get me wrong I loved watching Tyler growing up and it is so precious to see your children as much as you can when they were young, but it was nice to get out, meet new people and earn a wage. I think a lot of women out there can relate to that.

About two years after getting the job, It was a Friday night and I finished at eight, I picked up Tyler's from Mums, I didn't stay as I was tired, it had been a long shift and I wanted a hot bath and tea and to watch some television. Mum had fed Tyler and he was already in his pyjamas and we went home.

We got in and the house was dark, I turned on the hall light and Tyler was tried, just holding onto me. I led him upstairs and put him into bed, kissed him good night and then I ran a bath. I had a lovely bath and when I was drying myself I realized I had come on my period. I'm pretty regular but I am heavy. At this time I wasn't on the pill or any contraception as there no one in my life, there hadn't been since Ian, one man and one baby! The doctor had said that I did have a slight iron deficiency but nothing that some greens in the diet wouldn't help at this stage. I used a tampon as I normally would and put on my dressing gown and went downstairs. I know this seemed detailed but it will all make sense in a bit. You asked that I give you as much detail as possible, so that we can get back into the moment.

I made some noodles, made a cup of tea, ate, smoked and watched some T.V. At around ten p.m. I heard Tyler up on the landing, so I got up, put the landing light on from the hallway switch at the bottom of the stairs and went up and Tyler's door was open and he was asleep in his bed with his night light on next to him. Even at ten he loved his night light. I thought I must have imagined it or maybe mistook a noise next door for a noise in our house, we live in a detached house next to an elderly couple, sometimes you can hear them doing things, moving furniture or something, rare but you can hear them. I go back down stairs and at the bottom of the stairs I felt a chill, like I had walked through a cold draught. I went back into the living room and sat back down on the sofa and again I hear footsteps on the landing. I turned the volume on the T.V right down and listened and clearly you could hear something on the landing. Like someone walking across it and opening the bathroom door and putting on the bathroom light. It had to be Tyler so I got up put on the landing light again and headed up the stairs. As I went up the stairs I walked through this draught again, like it was moving up the stairs with me. I remember my arms and legs were covered in goose bumps and my neck hairs were standing on end, I got upstairs and again Tyler was in bed and I quietly went into his room and he was fast asleep. The bathroom door was shut and the when I opened the door to double check the light was off in there.

When you are tired you imagine some strange things and when you're a woman living on your own with your ten year old son you can worry about burglars and intruders. I always keep a hammer next to my bed in case someone breaks in, in the night and sadly in this area there have been quite a number of burglaries over the years.

I went back down stairs this time the cold spot was not there and I double checked that the front door and the back door were locked. The house is comprised of two floors. The front door leads to a hallway that leads to a small kitchen. To the right as you come in is a flight of stairs that leads to the landing with the bathroom straight ahead, two larger bedrooms to your left and a small box room opposite the bathroom. Leading off the hallway is a living room that faces the street and a back dining room that faces the garden. The garden is only small but it was big enough to have a washing line and a slide for Tyler when he was little. I was never one for gardening but I'd mow the lawn a couple of times in the summer and sit out there with Mum and have a beer. The elderly people next door were nice enough and they grew their own food and now and again the old man would hand me some spuds, tomatoes or spring onions. Once he gave us some rhubarb and I had no clue what to with that, I gave it to mum who made Rhubarb and ginger jam.

So back to that night and the house is secure and I'm tired, I go up to bed but before I go into my bedroom I go for a wee and brush my teeth and I'm sat there brushing them and I feel this overpowering nervousness, I have a ball in my stomach, a feeling of dread that someone is watching me, that if I open the bathroom door that someone will be stood there in the dark. I can't explain how I got the feeling; perhaps it was just anxiety from hearing all the noises upstairs and there being nothing there. It took a lot to open that bathroom door I can tell you. I opened it up and nothing, just the light from my room from across the landing. I pop my head into to see that Tyler is still sound asleep, and he is. I go into my room and close my door. I close the door tight as sometimes I use toys on myself and I don't want Tyler to see or hear me now that would scar the lad besides I was single and a woman has needs. No woman should feel ashamed of pleasuring herself and it's safer than just going out and bringing random men into your home. I don't like that but I didn't masturbate this night as I was tired and on my period and I just went to bed. I normally wear a small blue night dress and I definitely did that night, I won't forget that night for as long as I live. I liked the blue night dress, it was comfortable, and I didn't sweat as much in it.

I woke at 2:40 a.m., that was the time on my clock radio and I don't know why I woke but I was just wide awake. My bedroom is painted blue but it was just an orange colour from where the outside street light was peering through my curtains, Just streaks of orange light across the room. I lay there and listened and nothing. I thought that perhaps Tyler had been up in the night and had flushed the toilet or something. I lay there and heard nothing and tried to get back to sleep, as I was dosing, I heard my bedroom door click like someone had just closed it. I jumped up and turned on the light and looked at the door and it was closed tight. I got up and opened the door and there was nothing on the landing just the pale light from the night light from Tyler's room and the light flooding in from behind me, my shadow actually made me jump. My heart was pounding in my ears.

As I left my room and stepped on the landing I was engulfed in a massive cold chill, absolutely freezing, from head to foot and as if it were in the core of my being, I dashed into Tyler's room, I was really scared. He was asleep and I thought I must have had a bad dream or misheard something natural in the house like the boiler or the house just settling. I often heard things in the attic and my mind was just playing tricks as it does when you're tired. You can actually scare yourself, you can convince yourself that something is there, you can give yourself the chills and goose bumps if you let yourself go with the fear. Most of us have done it at some stage. I remember once being on an overnight school trip and we had been talking about ghosts and in particular the Black Nun which was said to haunt the dormitory's there and in the night I had to go to the loo and because we had been scaring each other I was shitting myself thinking of crossing that landing to use the loo and that the Black Nun would get me and that was how I felt on this night. I was simply scaring myself.

I was tired and I went back into my room and had to cover my mouth to stifle a scream. Where I had pushed the duvet off me in my panic to get the light on, the white sheets were stained with my blood, but not just a patch of blood but a long trailing handprint from the middle of the sheets all the way down to the bottom of the bed. You could clearing identify a hand, a big hand like a man's, five longs fingers spread apart with trails of my blood all the way down like someone had put their fingers inside me and wiped my menstrual blood all the way down the sheets.

I quickly checked myself and the tampon was still in and there was not a mark on me not a speckle on my underwear or my night dress. Nothing but these long bloody finger marks all the way to the bottom of the bed. I panicked and I ripped the sheets from the bed, ran downstairs sobbing and flung them into the washing machine. I know I should have kept them, taken a photo or something, called the police but can you imagine how it feels to see that in your bed? The sheets had been washed and were like new when I put them on the bed. How can you explain it? My tampon was still in place, my underwear was till on, I hadn't been raped, that I could tell. There was no one in the house. I couldn't let my baby boy see this. What would you do? Who would you tell?

I washed those sheets and I sat in the kitchen smoking and crying. I was in such a state. I didn't dare go back to bed that night and I just lay on the settee with the TV on waiting for the dawn. Those long bloody smear marks chill me to this day. I knew then there was something in this house, something non-human, a ghost or something, it had been watching and following me around the house all night. I knew it was there, just knew it and as soon as I was asleep it snuck into the room with me and it had put itself inside me and I had been violated.

Haunting

Lisa takes a deep drag on her cigarette and looks briefly away from me as if she is ashamed of what she has told me. Few people outside her inner circle have been privy to this disturbing account. She knows now she has committed herself to divulge the atrocity that has been forced upon her. However, perhaps like you have after reading that, I have my doubts. I probe further asking could it have been possible that it was a person in the house or perhaps she had done it herself in a slumbering sleep like trance. Sleepwalkers exhibit the most unusual behaviour and great study and research has been conducted into this, documenting and recording some extraordinary extracurricular nocturnal activity. Lisa's eyes flash with anger and she scolds me, reminds me that I have not had to live in this house, she is the one who has been victim of this transgression, and she is the one that has been violated. I apologise for seeming somewhat conventional in my thinking but it is from necessity, I have to look at this from every angle and examine every detail. She calms, understanding the nature of my inquisitiveness and I have to remind myself that this woman has been the victim of abuse for perhaps decades. I focus her back on the events leading to the first full on metaphysical contravention, which took place six years after the first infraction. In this section I have merged interviews from both Lisa and Tyler in a chronological order so you can get a clearer understanding of the abnormal and uncompressible events that took place.

Lisa: I understand your doubts about the night with the finger marks. I do, but I didn't do it, no one else was in the house and if some sick bastard out there thinks somehow my ten year old son was responsible then they can fuck off. There was something in that house that night, it was following me around, it was spying on me and I panicked and washed the sheets. I called Mum in the morning and she took it as naturally as if I had spilt some milk. She said not to worry that it hadn't harmed Tyler or me and that she would pop over and sort it after she had finished at her arts and crafts class. I was furious, I was crying on the phone. What am I to do? Call the police? Dial 999 and say a ghost put its fingers in my vagina while I was on my period and rubbed them all over the bed sheets? They would have taken Tyler from me and locked me up in a loony bin. I was scared.

Tyler: I remember that day, Mum was on the phone crying and I didn't know then what is was about. I can't remember anything about that night, Mum told me in later years and it just made me so sick, so angry but worse was yet to come. It got real bad.

Lisa: Mum came over in the afternoon and she gave me a hug and she went into the Kitchen and made us a cuppa. I admit I felt better for her being there, I told her what happened. Tyler was in his room playing on his computer games so I told her everything. Mum said it would be O.K. and said she would bless the house and it won't happen again and off she went blessing the house. She had incense sticks and candles and she chanted away. She then opened all the windows and said a hushed prayer and she said to me it was all good and that Tyler and I would be happy now nothing would harm us, nothing would bother us and just to move on and forget about it. I was still scared that night, I slept with the light on and nothing happened, nor the next night or the night after that, in fact nothing happened for years.

Lisa: A few years after Mum blessed the house little things started to happen. Nothing serious but little things, which in hindsight might be related. Things some people, that are sceptical, can easily explain away. But you have asked that I remember as much detail as possible no matter how small. That house was quite a modern build, I'm not sure maybe the fifties, but the council had been there over the years fixing the guttering or installing new heating or electrics. The house was pretty much well looked after and I always kept it clean and tidy and Tyler is as good as gold always tidying up after himself, it's good that he has pride himself that way. Anyway, one night I'm in bed and I hear a big thud up above me, I was just dropping off and it did frighten me. I sat up and I thought that maybe one of Tyler's old toys or a box of Christmas decorations had fallen over up there. It was around 11 p.m. and I just thought it is what it is and there's nothing more I can do and that I will have a look in the morning before work.

I lie back down and a few minutes later another thud and I'm thinking what the shit is that? Maybe a bird is nesting up there, but then I think perhaps the old neighbours are putting things in their attic and it's just the noise from that. So I ignore it again and a few moments later directly above me another big thud. I sat up and put on the light, put on my dressing gown, headed onto the landing and stood under the attic door. I think I half expected to see the attic door fly open and some grey skinny arms reach out towards me. Nothing happened and I went back to bed and there was nothing more that night.

Tyler: One night, I was about eleven I think, I was in bed and I saw the landing light on through the crack in my door. I could hear someone on the landing. I got up and mum was stood there just staring up at the ceiling. I asked her what time it was and she told me to hush, she just grabbed my hand and she held it so hard, she was so cold to the touch. I asked again, she just shook me and hushed me again. Then I heard it. In the attic we kept all my old toys. All my toddler stuff and one of them was a plastic piano, battery operated and you could hear it playing upstairs. It was right above us. Not the auto beat or a programmed tune, just two or three chords played slowly and deliberately. It was Dum Duh Duh, Dum Duh Duh. Like a sad slow old song. I asked mum again, she looked at me cross and the noise stopped. She sent me back to bed, when I asked her about it in the morning she said she had taken care of it and there were three or four rubbish bags in the hall. She said not to tell Nan and that it wouldn't happen again.

Lisa: I know we live in a built up council estate but we are towards the end of this one and it's a dead end. You can hear cars and occasionally you can hear an ambulance or a police car in the distance, but we are at the end of the street and we are attached to some old people that we never really hear. At the end of our road are some fields and woods. In the summer, if the windows are open, you can hear Barbeques and parties from people in the street, but it's a peaceful enough place. That night with the toy piano upstairs, I woke up thinking I could hear a radio or something on, I heard this tune playing upstairs in the attic. I was terrified and after what had happened before with the bloody finger-marks I started to think maybe this house was really haunted and that Mum hadn't helped at all. I must have stood on that landing for twenty minutes just listening to that tune with my spine tingling and all my hair stood up on end. Tyler woke up and we stood there and listened till it stopped. I put him back to bed and I went back to my room. I found it so hard to sleep, I just lay on my back starring at the ceiling and imagining all this crazy shit happening up there. I imagined ghosts creeping around, messing with Tyler's old toys and the things we kept up there. I imagined them listening to us, laughing at us that they scared us so much, that as soon as it got dark they would come out and haunt us. I eventually fell into an uneasy sleep that night and woke up that morning and it was about seven. Tyler was still asleep and I thought I could give him longer today as he woke up in the night. I went to the loo and thought, fuck it, this is my house, if things want to piss about then I'll make it hard for them. When you're tired and scared you think some strange thoughts.

I got dressed and I went up in the attic and cleared most of it out. Tyler wouldn't need his old toys anymore and I wasn't planning on having any more kids, besides, if I did then I would just get new things. While I was up there I found the little toy piano, under a bin bag full of Christmas tinsel. I picked it up expecting it to start playing or to be freezing cold or something odd but nothing happened. I turned it over and the panel on the back where the batteries went was missing and there were no batteries in it. There was no other toy like it up there and people can say that maybe it somehow retained its charge but really? It would play for twenty minutes on a bit of charge? I binned it, binned all of the old toys. I threw them into bin bags and chucked them out for the bin men. We never heard the piano again up there.

Tyler: After the piano in the attic night, I remember waking up in the night and I could hear someone singing. I thought Mum had the T.V on. At this time she didn't have a boyfriend and it was just us two. I thought maybe it was the old man next door. I listened for ages to this singing. I couldn't make out the words but I definitely heard it. I got up and stood on the landing and I could hear it above me in the attic. I got frightened and I went into mum's room, I was really scared and mum was just sat there with the light on looking at the ceiling. She looked at me and motioned for me to come to her and I just hugged her and she held me there stroking my hair. She was shaking and we both waited there on the bed and then the singing suddenly stopped. I slept in Mums room that night. It was such a creepy experience. It gives me goose bumps now telling you about it. I know worse things have happened but that was so creepy.

Lisa: The singing in the attic was a slow sad song. It was a man singing it, I'm sure of that, it was like those songs they sang in the olden days. Queen Victoria days. It was really slow and sad. I couldn't make out the words but you could hear it upstairs in the cold and dark attic. Thinking of that night makes me feel so sad. I'm not sure if it's just because whatever was up there was spreading sadness through the house, into Tyler and my life or because I realised things were never really going to be happy in this house, that we were not alone. Tyler was really brave that night; I have no idea what I would have done without my brave little man. I was tempted to just take him and go to Mums but part of me didn't want to admit to mum I was scared. I knew if I talked to her about all this that she would just say that's it ok, that we live close to the spirit world and these events, this haunting was just as natural as breathing, plus she would just do another blessing. I didn't want her here, involved all the time as I knew she loved it, she relished all of this. It was proof enough to her that she was right. It sounds selfish but I didn't want her to have that proof. I didn't want her to be right. I just wanted a life without ghosts and aliens and angels and the supernatural. I wanted a Normal life with Tyler. I know there was naughty boy when Rose and I were little but we were little and who knows what we saw and felt back then, it was a long time O.K? Maybe I thought the finger marks were something else, maybe somehow I had done it. I didn't want a haunted house, I just wanted a warm and bright home for me and my son and any parent out there I hope would want the same. What I wanted and what I got were two very different things though.

Tyler: I just remembered that before anything strange would happen I would hear a ticking like a clock in the living room. We didn't have a clock in there but you would hear it for a few minutes and then that same day or night something strange would happen. It was just a tick, tick, tick. I heard a clock like it in an old antiques shop I popped into when I needed furniture for my flat but it was far too expensive in there. In there was an old brown wooden clock, it had a round face and the numbers were in a roman style and I listened to it for ages as it reminded me of the ticking I could hear at Mums over those years. The man there said it was fifty pounds and that it was made in the nineteen twenties. I should have bought it but it was too expensive for me, nearly a week's rent for a clock. Maybe I should have found out more about it but then again maybe it was just a clock. You look for answers all the time after you have experienced what we have. You look for clues and connections anything that could help give us answers. You see horror movies where an item is returned and the hauntings stop or they find a body and give it a burial and it finds peace and the ghost is thankful and

never returns. You look for things like that, that is why
we contacted you. Maybe you or someone reading this
will be able to help us understand what has been
happening to us. Maybe someone out there reading this
knows exactly what is happening and can tell us how to
end this. One thing I think about a lot about these early
days is, what kind of ghost sits up in an attic singing and
playing Piano? Why would it do that? What a fucking
weirdo.

Lisa: I have never heard a ticking in this room but Tyler
said he has heard it and some other people said they
have. Strange that I have been here all this time and
never heard it.

Tyler: When I was about thirteen, Mum was downstairs
watching T.V and I was in the bath and in the bathroom
the room filled up with the smell of shit, like that really
bad smell I smelt when I was a kid and the room went
icy cold. It was awful, I thought the drains were blocked,
I was nearly sick. I got out of the bath and put on a towel
and I unlocked the bathroom door and I went to open it
and it was still locked, I checked the lock, the smell was
suffocating by now and the cold was so intense but the
door could not open. I had to yank the handle down and
as soon as I stepped foot on the landing the cold and
smell were gone. I half expected Mum to be stood there
holding the handle as a joke or something but she

wasn't. She's not much of a prankster to be honest. It reminded me of the day I thought I saw that smelly dirty man on top of the stairs. By this time I was convinced without a shadow of a doubt that the house was haunted.

Lisa: As Tyler got older I started working more shifts to get money in. Tyler was eating me out of house and home and he always needed new trainers or a new video game or something or other but as I said I didn't mind working at all, I really enjoyed it there. I met some new friends and I get to deal with the public a lot. One guy would come in and be friendly and chat with me. He was very handsome and one night, on a staff girls' night out, I met him. He bought me a drink and was very complimentary towards me. His name was Leon, he was a bit older than me, a short Mediterranean looking guy with loads of amazing tattoos and we just hit it off. He was working down here on the refineries and was from up north, he had no family down here and he asked me on a date. I hadn't been on a date in years! Not since Ian all those years back. People can judge me all they want, but I put Tyler first all those years. I saw Leon a few times and one night we went for dinner, we had some wine and I asked him back to mine. Tyler was staying over at Mums, I would not dare bring anyone home while Tyler was there. Not that I was ashamed of him or anything as I was very open that I had a son and that I had been on my own for years, but it was not fair on Tyler to see men coming home, sharing my bed, leaving in the morning. I always thought if it worked out proper then I would introduce Tyler and maybe have a day out together so we could all get along.

Anyway, I took Leon home and we were sat on the sofa, he said to me, can I kiss you? I just melted and we kissed. It was an amazing feeling to be desired again even if he just wanted me for one thing, I could live with that. I took him upstairs and I thought it's been so long that it's probably scabbed up! Only messing, I'd be O.K as I had been using my vibrator that week in anticipation! It was amazing, it was worth the wait and he was so passionate and so experienced. He did things to me that I had never had done to me before. The last time that I had intimacy like that I was just a teenager, it was clumsy and rough, now I was a woman and he treated me like one. After we came, I lay there and he got up to use the loo, he came back and asked if there was anyone else in the house. I said no, that I wouldn't have made the noises I did if there were and I asked 'why?' He said he thought he'd saw a man popping into the other bedroom. I said that was strange and we both went and checked. There was no one there, I checked the front and back door and both were locked. Mum and Tyler have a spare key but no one else. I was tempted to give one to the neighbours but I chose not to. Guess I didn't like the thought that an old man could snoop around my house while I was in work and Tyler was in school.

Leon and I got on well. It was easy. I would pop over to his in the week on his day off and about once a fortnight he would come over to mine when Mum had Tyler. He was a good man, easy going; quiet, liked his beer and his video games but he always had time for me. One night he came over and we had dinner, watched a movie and went to bed. In the morning I was sat naked having a wee on the loo when this icy coldness overwhelmed me like before, the night with the finger marks and an overpowering stench, like someone had emptied their innards on the floor. It was disgusting. I'm sat there, covered in goose bumps and holding my nose trying to pee quicker, when Leon walks in, makes an awful face, holds his nose and says that I should lock the door if I'm having a dump! He thought it was me. I was mortified. I finished up and as soon as I got on the landing the smell and the cold just vanished. I said nothing to Leon but I started thinking no, not know, the thing from before was back. I finally decided to approach mum about the events in the house and spoke to Mum quickly when I went to pick up Tyler. She said not to worry it was probably just coincidence and she would pop over and put a plaster on the house. She meant she would do another blessing.

Tyler: When I was about fifteen I was sat in the living room watching T.V, it was a Friday night as Mum was out with her fella Leon. He was a nice guy; he was into video gaming so we had something in common. I was sat on the settee with my legs stretched out across it and it was summer so I was just in my shorts and there was this weird ringing noise in my ear, like if you listen to music too loud, like a high pitched noise. I put my finger in my ear as I thought I could just jiggle it out but then I realised that the noise was in the room and not in my head. I thought it was something outside in the street, like a truck or engineers working on something like the phone line and then this weird static feeling covers me and all the hairs stood up on my legs and on my arms. I couldn't move for a few seconds and then it just passed. I get a chill thinking about that sensation now as it felt like a weird electrical static just passed through me. I was a little freaked out but I thought I can't do anything and just carried on watching T.V. About an hour later I got up to get some lemonade from the kitchen and as I was going back into the room I saw a little ball of blue light just pass across the room. It was definitely there as it passed the mirror, it reflected, it made a few spiralling motions and then just vanished into the ceiling. A mate of mine is an electrician and he reckons that the whole thing might have been an electrical charge building up in the room and creating a little energy orb. He says it can happen. I saw a program on discovery about ball lightening and it could have been that but after that night I noticed a few odd little things start to happen.

Lisa: One night Leon and I were in bed. I woke up and the bedroom door opened and someone went onto the landing and I heard the bathroom light go on. It's on a string and it makes a clunk noise when pulled. I lay there dozing thinking that Leon was up using the loo when next to me I heard a small cough and Leon was In bed next to me. I even put my arm on him and it was him. I put on the bedside lamp and looked at him sleeping and I stood out of bed and I heard the bathroom light go off and I went onto the landing and there was nothing there. I thought maybe it was Tyler but there was no one there. I turned on the landing light and opened the bathroom door and the light string was just slowly spinning. I checked that no one was in there. It might have been a draught and maybe I dreamt it all but when I turned to go back into my bedroom I felt that coldness again and I felt sick. Thankfully Tyler was older probably about fifteen and Leon was there so I felt safer. I went to bed and prayed that it was just nothing, just a dream. I was angry as Mums quick fixes were having no affect.

Tyler: I don't know why but it always seems that these hauntings happen at night. It was a Friday night again about 10pm I was sat in my room playing video games when I hear this low mumbling. It was real low, like two men chatting. Mum and Leon are out and I turn down the T.V. I can honestly say I have never heard the neighbours. I have never as they are so old and quiet and keep themselves to themselves. I don't know if they can hear us, I hope not after some of the girls I have had over. The T.V is right down and I stand up and it sounds like two men are having a conversation on the landing. I shit myself, I panicked and grabbed a dumbbell from the side of the bed and headed towards the door. I was really into my weights back then. I thought someone had broken in, it has happened in our street before and it definitely wasn't Mum and Leon. As I got closer to the door I could hear two men having a row, but quietly, all hushed and whispered. It was barely audible but you could hear it. I did not want to open that door and I put my hand the door handle and it was so cold, like when you freeze burn yourself with a can of deodorant, when it's too close to your skin. I was bricking it, whoever was behind that door was going to get the dumbbell to the head and I would deal the consequences later. I grabbed a sock off my dresser to put on the door handle and as I went to open the door again I head a man shout *"LEAVE IT!"* I jumped and I swung open the door and there was no one there. No one but I could have sworn that the men were on the landing. I ran downstairs. The front door and back door locked, I checked the whole house.

There was no one in mums room or the box room or anywhere in the house. Then I thought, they are in the fucking attic! Maybe someone had broken in next door and was now trying to get into ours. There is a ladder leading to the attic and I pulled it down and I must have built myself up for a minute or two before I went up there as I was shitting it and it's hard to climb a ladder with a dumbbell. I got up and I just hurled the attic door upwards and darted my arm in there to find the light, I turned it on and peeped in and there was nothing but the beams and old Christmas decorations and the yellow lagging. There was a red brick wall separating our side of the house from the other and I even checked it to see no bricks had been removed. I got a few fibre splinters in my bare feet but up there, there was nothing. As I headed back to the ladder, I hear it again, below me; two men talking in hushed voices. I looked down onto the landing and I can't see anyone there but I can hear them, just a few feet below me. I hear one thing, one thing so clearly that freaked me out. One of the voices said, *"He's listening."* And they stopped and I never heard them again. I got down from the attic and there was no one there. People can say it was people in the street or maybe it was the neighbours but these voices, whispering but angry and hissing were just a few feet from me and they were aware I was there and I think that was the part that frightens me most of all, the fact that they were aware of me. I thought ghosts just were oblivious to us, just walking through walls and moving shit about. I wish I had heard more of what they were saying, what did one of them mean by *leave it?*

Lisa: It wasn't till years later that I heard about Tyler's experience that night with the voices but Leon and I both heard those. I'm convinced we heard the same thing. Tyler was at my mums or out playing football one evening and Leon and I had a shower and we felt a little frisky and we nipped into my room for a quickie. I loved sex with Leon, it was always so passionate, and he really knew how to please me. We came, we often came together and we were just lying there with him on top of me and we were panting and kissing and then out of nowhere I thought I heard voices on the landing. I thought, shit Tyler's home and he's probably heard us both shagging. Leon rolled off me and hid under the duvet and I could hear him giggling and I pulled the duvet up over my chest too. I lay there and I called to Tyler a few times and no reply, I thought I must have imagined it. Leon was being naughty and touching me under the duvet while I was trying to be all serious and concerned, but there was no one there. I lay back down and faced Leon, our faces close together, we held each other. We were all clammy and sweaty from the sex and we hear the voices again, quiet but close, not from outside in the street but by the bedroom door. I'm just about to get up when I hear someone shout *"MINE!"* It was really loud, like a gunshot. It was a shock and it frightened us both so much, that's how loud it was. Leon and I shot out of bed and put on our dressing gowns, there was no one on the landing, no one in the house. I am sure that it was two men talking in angry voices and what did they mean by *MINE*?, I think one of them was cross that Leon was having sex with me, as time went on I think the ghost got more and more jealous of my partners. But all of these things, these happenings were nothing compared to what it would do next.

Intrusion

Lisa asks for a few moments for preparation, to compose herself, before she is to continue with her story. I take my leave along with the female psychologist who has joined us for this session; we leave the smell of Tabaco and coffee in the living room and stand in the fresh air of the garden. It is a beautiful day with a blue sky with the sun behind the house casting long shadows across the lawn and fence. In the fresh air I digest the information which I have been given and I try to make sense of the people who live here and their perception of the events. I have pushed Lisa hard, trying to extract as much information as possible always examining her body language and her tone of voice. My initial reaction is whatever has happened to Lisa, she does believe has occurred. If she believes this to be true, then I have to determine whether this is psychological, or in fact a haunting. I have a very passive aggressive interview style, I appear unassuming but in every word I am looking for clues. Every question is designed to muster as much detail as possible and from the detail I can zero in on the truths or the inconsistencies of the account. I do have doubts about Tyler, I feel that there is something he is hiding or dreading to reveal. I will have to delve deeper into Tyler's story, I need to bring this element to the surface. Something has happened to him and I begin to fear the worse. What if, what had happened to his mother, the sexual violation, the carnal wrong doing, had also happened to him? I needed answers but I had to be sensitive in my approach. I turn around and Lisa is stood in the kitchen window. She has a reluctant smile; she knows that everything we have discussed so far is easy, compared to this. I often have an emotional disconnection so I can focus exclusively on the witness's account, but for those brief seconds, as I look back at her, I feel a melancholy for her. All she wanted was a good life for her and her son. She had no expectation of grandeur or of wealth, just of happiness. Please be warned that this part of the investigation contains graphic sexual description and events of an extremely disturbing and chilling nature. Caution is advised.

Lisa: At this time I was convinced that perhaps there were two spirits in the house. The reason I thought this is because there seemed to be a smelly, nasty one and then a sad shy one. Perhaps they were arguing all the time; maybe one was trying to protect me from the other. I'm not sure. Mum seemed to think that maybe it was one spirit with multiple personalities. She said like Gollum in the Hobbit films. That did nothing to relax me at all. In fact it made me more afraid, because with my reasoning at least there was one out there trying to protect me. Tyler had heard two men arguing and so did Leon and me.

Talking of Leon, He got called away up north as his mum took ill, he went up and I never saw him again. I was heartbroken. We spoke on the phone and he said he'd had enough of Pembrokeshire and that he wanted to be home, closer to his family and friends up there. I pleaded that we could perhaps do long distance or maybe I could move up there, anything I could do to keep him in my life but he said no. He said things were complicated but that we could be friends and who knew what would happen in the future, he never kept in touch and eventually I stopped texting. I stopped believing.

I was in shock. I loved him so much and for the first time since Ian, I opened up. I let myself fall madly in love. It was like losing a limb. There was a big empty hole in me and whenever I thought of him that hole would seep a cold sorrow into my heart. I cried and cried as in my heart and mind we would make it, be a family and be together forever. I was so upset that I took a week off work. I was a shambles. Everywhere I went in my home there were memories haunting me of Leon, He had left quickly and without warning. There were clothes of his still at mine. His aftershave, deodorant's and tooth brush were a constant reminder in the bathroom. The bedroom smelled of him. In the kitchen sat his cup I got him for valentines. All the things he had bought and treated me too were like anchors of what we had and how I could not let go. I just couldn't believe it was over, I just hoped he would call me and say he was coming home and we would start again. I didn't want an apology or an explanation. I just wanted him to hold me and kiss me the way he did. I never asked anything of him, I thought we had something easy, something special. I didn't put any pressure on him, I was considerate to his needs and I just prayed every day for so long that he would text or call. That call never came. Like Ian he just vanished. It is a hard thing to lose someone you love so much, my advice to anyone out there that truly loves someone, is not to take it for granted. I know women that are insecure and stubborn and have lost good men because of it. The men loved them, but were given no choice but to leave, they felt pushed out and isolated.

Just hold on to those you love as you never know when you will lose them. Do anything it takes to hold onto it, even if it means admitting your wrong or that you have issues and you need that support, you want that love. Life can be very lonely without the love of a good man. I know this more than anyone.

 About two months after Leon left me I went out on a work night out with some of the Girls. They are fabulous. They tried so hard to cheer me up but I had that sadness within and I wasn't interested in finding another man or having a one night stand. I sat most of the night watching them dance and flirt and they beckoned me over wanting me to join in but I sat there and drank. One of my friends found me in the toilet crying and she just hugged me and said a good dance would help. I went on the dance floor and just stood there bawling as everyone danced around me. I must have looked a right state. The girls wanted to get a minibus to Haverfordwest as there were a few night clubs there but I just was too sad to go and I felt I was just bringing everyone down. I just wanted to go home. Tyler was about sixteen at this time and he was at a mates or a girl's house. He had a girlfriend around this time. I can't remember her name. I don't think they lasted long. I just hoped he didn't get her knocked up like me and his Dad had. Not that I begrudged Tyler at all, he was my life, and I just wanted him to live a little before he settled down.

Tyler spent more and more time away, given some of the things that had happened in the house I couldn't blame him, but I wanted the company. Sometimes it's just nice to know that there is someone else in the house with you. They don't even have to be in the same room, but it is comforting knowing they are there. I just felt the need to go home, after all, I had drank quite a bit and some fat sweaty man had been trying it on with me, that depressed me even more, thinking that only a fat sweaty man would be interested in me! Back then I had a great figure, when I made the effort I looked good, I definitely didn't need the attention of some overweight drunk. I was always confident in how I looked, just not confident with how to talk to men. I think you can understand why that is. They all have a habit of just disappearing out of my life with no warning. Leon did all the work in the early days, he did all the flirting, chatting and chasing. I liked it as he made it easy for me. I guess I am shy.

I got home and was relieved; it was a big step going out for the first time after he left. It can go one of two ways; either you're a miserable mess reeking of Bensons and heartache or you become a dancing, drinking, pulling machine. Well that's what I've noticed in myself anyway.

That night I was utterly depressed, home was a familiar and welcoming place to be, even if I was home alone.

I took off my heels and tights and pulled my dress off over my head. I sat in the living room in just my bra and knickers, drank a pint of water and smoked a cigarette. The curtains were closed, I think it was about eleven thirty, perhaps twelve, I was shattered. I stood up, turned off the living room light and went into the hallway, as I was about to turn the landing light on, I could have sworn that I saw someone stood on the landing. It looked like a figure of a man. Just briefly in the corner of my eye. I thought it might have been Tyler, maybe he had fallen out with his girlfriend or something and had come home. I shouted up for Tyler, but no reply, I turned on the light and there was nobody there. I was drunk and tired and just wanted a pee, brush my teeth and fall into bed. There was no one on the landing, I checked Tyler's room and he was not there.

I sat on the loo brushing my teeth when I suddenly went deathly cold. A chill spread all over my body, like a freezing cold draught. I just told myself to ignore it, push it away and the feeling will go away. I was passed caring to be honest. Ghosts or no ghosts I had a terrible night on the town and an awful couple of months with Leon abandoning me. The feeling quickly passed so I thought *see, nothing* and I literally fell into bed. I unhooked my bra and flung it across the room, turned off the light and fell asleep.

I woke in the night all confused and disorientated. You know when you don't know where you are, or what time it is and I think I had been dreaming of Leon. I noticed that I was wet between the legs. I was warm and wet and thought I must have been having a wet dream but then I realised then something was flicking against my clit. Something wet but freezing cold. I panicked and thought that someone was in the house. This wasn't a dream. I could not move, I could not move a muscle and there was a rushing sound in my ears. I couldn't scream, I couldn't turn my head, I couldn't do anything.

I was convinced that there was someone giving me oral sex, lapping at my clit, I thought that maybe I had been spiked and that someone had followed me home and broken in and was now raping me. I was terrified. I was paralysed. I could not even scream. I felt a cold finger push itself inside me, like a man's finger, it was inside me not rough but gentle and it slid in and out of me in a gentle motion all the while my clit was being licked. It wasn't forceful but it was freezing cold and that was uncomfortable in itself, I could not see obviously as it was dark and I was frozen but that is what it felt like. I couldn't feel a head or the shoulders of a person between my legs, or someone lying on me, or close to me. The fingering and the licking stopped and for this I was so thankful. I tried to sit up, to kick and lash out, but still I was paralysed. I just lay there motionless. I couldn't even cry and I had thoughts of Tyler coming in and seeing his mum being raped. How awful that would be for him. I just prayed that whatever drugs were used on me would wear off or that whoever was doing this would get up and leave. Maybe panic that they were taking too long and leave. I thought as soon as they are gone that I would call the police, call my mum, and just get help from anyone. Over and over in my mind I hoped that Leon would miss me and turn up and rescue me.

I felt icy breath close to my skin moving up my body and then I felt a cold kiss on my nipple. There was a cold tongue, icy lips and breath on my tit and it just suckled on my right breast for what felt like an eternity. There was no arousing sensation like when you have sex, it was so bitterly cold. There was no pressure on me, no weight of a person, just this cold icy breath moving across my body. The cold breath made its way up to my mouth, the cold air touched my lips, filled my mouth and lungs and I felt something penetrate inside my vagina. A cold icy penis, big and hard, throbbing, thrusting and pushing while cold air filled my mouth and air rushed in my ears. It went on forever, deep penetrating thrusts. I feel so ashamed but I started to orgasm, I could feel my vagina clasping onto its cock even though I was numb down there with the cold and then the head of its cock swelled and just when I thought I was about to cum everything stopped. Everything just stopped; from the feeling of cold air in my mouth, the rushing air in my ears, the feeling of a penis inside me. Everything just stopped. I reached for the light, turned it on and lept out of bed. I actually fell out of bed as I was tangled up in the duvet, I lay on the floor in a heap and looked around the room. The bedroom door was shut tight and I could not see anyone under the bed from where I was. I was wrapped up in the duvet and the bed was empty. My heart was racing and pounding in my ears. I found the courage to stand up and check the room. Nothing was there. I even checked the wardrobe and the bedroom windows but they were locked from the inside. There was no one in the room.

I grabbed the hammer from under the bed and I ran on to the landing, I was actually shouting. I think I shouted things like, *How fucking dare you touch me and I'll kill you, I'll kill you if you touch me again.* I was furious. I checked the house and the doors were locked, Tyler was not in his room, not at home. In the living room is a big mirror as you can see and I just stood starring at it. I was naked but my knickers were still on as they were when I went to bed, I felt myself down there, I was numb and wet. I felt like I'd had sex. I sat down on the settee and cried. I was so angry, so confused. Had I been raped?

There was no one in the house, yet I had felt, what I thought, was a tongue licking my clit. I felt a finger inside me, I felt breath, lips and a tongue on my nipple, a penis inside me. I felt like any longer and I would have cum. I felt so awfully ashamed. What if I had cum? What kind of person would it make me, to find pleasure in a violation like that? I felt, despite what my mind and heart felt, that my body had betrayed me by enjoying the sensation. It was all so confusing. The time was only 1 a.m., I had been in bed about an hour. It happened all so quickly.

I was about to call the police when I thought *what am I going to tell them*? That I went out, got pissed, came home, was paralysed and some invisible man had sex with me? They would just think I was some nutter, some piss head having a laugh and would arrest me for wasting police time. I was grateful for one thing, that Tyler was not home. I could not bear to think of him seeing me like this, semi naked, make up all over my face, tears rolling down my cheeks.

I made a cigarette and I howled and howled. I knew what this was; I knew exactly what it fucking was. It was the ghost, it was the fucking ghost. It was the same dirty, cowardly prick that had put its fingers in me when I was on my period. I was so disgusted that I choked on the cigarette smoke and was sick all over the floor. I literally spewed on the floor. My life at this time, I felt, was a joke. No living man wanted to be with me and ghosts wanted to fuck me. I wished to be dead, that mum would look after Tyler. I was miserable and depressed beyond all belief; I was a victim of an illegal sexual act in my OWN home. If it wasn't for Tyler I would have ended it there, but I couldn't bear to leave him behind. I know that's a dark statement and many people out there would do anything to bring people they have lost back to life. People might think that wanting to throw away something as precious as a life is utterly wrong, but until they are in my situation, how could they possibly tell how they would react?

I thought maybe I'd had some breakdown. Maybe after everything with Leon, the strains and pressures of life, I had just gone mad. Or was it a vivid dream? I had heard that in your sleep you can freeze up and not be able to move, but this was so real. The feelings in my vagina and my breast and lips were real. I knew this much. Part of me almost hoped that I had gone mad or that maybe someone had spiked me with drugs which made me hallucinate. I have never taken any drugs, not even smoked weed or anything like that. I hate the idea of not being in control. I do drink, not a huge amount, I hate the hangovers and sickness associated with booze, but I have been very drunk from time to time. I knew that after all the years of hauntings and strange events in the house that the ghost had returned. The same one that fingered me all those years back.

I slowly made my way upstairs, one slow step at a time, terrified that it would be up there, just waiting for me. I was in a daze, shock I guess. I went into the bathroom, ran the shower and sat under the hot water. I wanted to wash it away from me, the experience, and the feelings. It was like every drop of warm water was removing the iciness of its touch. I guess, I hoped that this would wash away the memory. I don't know how long I was in there for, but I was startled to hear the door handle turning. I thought no, not again, just get away and I screamed *LEAVE ME ALONE, JUST FUCKING LEAVE ME ALONE!!!*

There was a silence and then a familiar voice called through the door; *Mum, Mum is everything O.K.?* It was Tyler. I have never been so happy in my life to hear someone's voice. I calmed myself, I was relieved and told him I was being sick and I would be out in a minute, bless him he asked if he could get me anything, he even asked if I wanted him to hold my hair. I don't think I could have loved him more at that point. I might have been abused and I might have lost my dignity but I still had my baby boy and my love for him.

I noticed that the light was bright outside. I had no idea how long I had been in the bathroom for. The water was freezing cold which I hadn't even noticed. The time was

9 a.m. I had sat in the bath under the shower for nearly eight hours. I clambered out of the bath. My head was aching, probably from the effects of the drink and the shock of what happened. I dried myself. I took off my knickers from the night before and put them in the bin in there. I never wanted to wear them or see them again as every time would remind me of the assault. I wrapped myself in a towel and headed onto the landing, bright and warm with the sun streaming in through the window. Tyler was in his room talking to someone on the phone; I darted into my bedroom, took the sheets and duvet off the bed and opened the windows wide to let the air and sunlight in. I wanted this room cleansed. I wanted the memory gone. While I was in there tidying I still, in some fucked up way, hoped to find some evidence that there had been a real physical intruder in the house, you know? So I could call the police and have someone deal with this. If I could find some evidence that a man had been here, then maybe I could prove that I wasn't going mad. There was no evidence. This ghost had been patient all those years, watching and lusting over me, gathering energy to abuse and frighten me, to sexually assault me, to treat me like a piece of meat. I hated its cowardice, that it paralysed me, used powers we can't comprehend, to rape me.

Broken, confused, violated and fighting the tears, I called Mum.

Judith

This paranormal account would not be complete without an interview with Lisa's mother herself. At this juncture of the investigation I need her insight on what she believed was happening to her only surviving daughter. Judith is a slight lady in her early sixties with long silver hair and a tremendous bright orange sun tan. She sits in her wicker chair staring at me. Her living room is a majestic spectacle of brightness, paintings, mirrors and a plethora of plants, all of which display colour and scent. The aroma of patchouli incense fills the room mingled with a hint of some herbal remedy perhaps tucked away in the roll up cigarette she drags on. Judith stares at me with a knowing gleam in her eye. She assumes I am sport. She bluntly challenges that I am a non-believer. She believes that I have come to her family to denounce the truth of supernatural existence. In her eyes I am a sceptic, with little regard for the reality of the events, here to chronicle the account for fun and ridicule for other non-believers.

She stares me in the eye and questions me regarding the validity of my knowledge of the supernatural. She asks what experience I have gained from hiding behind my notepad and typewriter. I sip on my green tea and I tell her. I tell her in a frank and candid manner. I explain to her that I have experienced and seen things in the last twenty five years that would send a sane person to an asylum. I explain to her that ninety five percent of the investigations I have conducted since I was eleven, had a perfectly rational explanation, however, it was the remaining five percent which haunted me, that lived in my dreams, waking me in the night gasping for breath and in the grips of panic. These unexplainable events fuelled me in my quest for the truth, to use my time on this Earth to try and find light in the darkness. I look her straight in the eye and tell her I have seen good and I have seen evil in this world. Whatever science thinks it knows, what we are told to believe, the simple fact of the matter is; mankind has no control over what passes from other dimensions, and planes of existence, into our world. I tell her this frightens me. I bluntly remind her not to confuse my objectivity for scepticism.

Satisfied she laughs and says *you're O.K. in my book*, she is now more than happy to speak to me. She muses that you cannot be sure in this day and age and claims that she knew I would be here and I had an important part to play in all this. She rolls another cigarette and our journey into her daughter's truly disturbing paranormal violation continues.

Judith: When Lisa called me the first time this all started to happen, I wasn't surprised at all. Our family is very close to the spirit world. Rose, my other daughter, who passed over thirty years ago, I still hear. Lisa has shut herself off so she does not see or hear these things. I think Tyler may be more in tune with the spirit world than he realises.

Rose's death at the time wracked me with such guilt and despair. You look back at that moment and you re-live it over and over in slow motion, always wishing I could have just held onto her hand, just spotted the car sooner, there are a million things you wish you can change but you can't. I blamed myself for my daughter being run over and killed.

Lisa had been sick that day, and stayed at home. Her father Paul was rarely home, but he was home that day, and I went out to pick up Rose. I walked to the school, as it was a glorious sunny day, and on my way picked up a bit of shopping. I met Rose at the school gates and there were lots of other mothers and children there, I enjoyed chatting to them and the bag of shopping I had started to tear and rip so I let go of Rose for one minute while I tried to sort it out. Her friend called her from the other side of the road, she ran across to see her and that was enough for her to be hit by a car. The stupid thing is, the car wasn't even going that fast. It hit her and she hit her head on the kerb. My baby girl was dead at eight and it was entirely my fault. People have said that it wasn't, but whose responsibility was it to get her home, and get her home safe? Whose responsibility is it to look after their own children?

Paul, my husband, was so cold towards me about it. He literally blamed me. When she was pronounced dead he slapped me in the face and said I had killed our little girl. He said I was not fit to have children and that they were not mere objects, not things that you lose or discard. I cried so hard and I can still feel the sting of pain on my face when he hit me, like a constant reminder of my failure as a mother. I ask any parent out there who reads this if they fully understand the grief and anguish of seeing your child on a cold metal slab? People have said that it is like they are sleeping. Not Rose, the wounds to her head and face were horrifying. The guilt, the pain, the anguish you feel, well nothing compares to that, nothing.

I must have near suffocated Lisa after that. I could not bear to let go of her, I am blessed that we still live as close as we do and I cherish the time I spend with her and Tyler. I was afraid they would leave and move up north with Leon, but thankfully that never happened. I wouldn't have let it happen. There are ways in life of stopping things, you know?

Paul left me not long after Rose's death. He left the air force and took a job away. I knew he had been having an affair for years, he took her with him and abandoned me and Lisa, alone with my grief and shame. Things had not been the same for us since the twins had been born. He said to me one night while he was drinking, that seeing me give birth to the twins had been the most disgusting thing he had ever witnessed. He couldn't bear to touch me or to have sex with me after that. He said to me that it made him wretch to think that he orally pleasured me and that my body was a mess afterwards, he said seeing me breast feed made him feel ill. I know the body is ravaged by childbirth but he was really disgusted by it all. I lied to Lisa for many years telling her how her Dad was not there to witness her birth, as the truth hurt me too much. I will tell her, not you, before this is all done. Childbirth is the most wondrous gift of nature and I was blessed to bring not just one life but two into this world, despite Paul's cruel words it *was* love that brought them into this world. When a relationship ends it is always easy to remember how it ended, how much you despise each other and have a hatred or loathing of that person. We often forget how good it is when we first meet, when we connect, and how great it feels the first night we make love.

I had fancied Paul for so long and when we had our first night together I just felt like pinching myself, I couldn't believe we were together. It was beautiful and some aspects of our time together have left a bitter taste in my mouth and a pain in my heart. I still hold on to those early times when we were truly in love and the fact that I had two beautiful girls.

About a year after Paul left, I was putting the washing out on the line. At this time I was exceptionally depressed. I had taken up drinking a huge amount, mainly rum, when Lisa had gone to bed I would just sit there in silence poring over old photo albums. Albums of my wedding day, shotgun of course as it was the done thing back in those days and pictures of the twins. From the day there were born to the last ever picture taken of Lisa and Rose, I kept them all. It's sad because when you see the picture of me holding the girls after they were born, you can see the exhaustion in my face, but also the true and incredible look of love and pride. Anyway, I was out putting the washing on the line and had an incredible hangover and I saw Lisa hiding behind a bed sheet I had put up. She was playing hide and seek with me and I could hear her giggling and see fleeting glimpses of her. I had left Lisa in the house and I thought the little monkey had snuck out, it did make me smile and it did cheer me up. I chased her around the washing, I was laughing my head off, it was such a tonic. I actually got caught up in some sheets and fell over. I lay there laughing and I could hear Lisa laughing too. I got up. Lisa was stood looking at me from the kitchen window smiling and waving at me. I was baffled and I looked around the washing expecting to see a neighbour's child, I thought they must have somehow climbed the fence and got into the garden, but there was no one there. I could have sworn it was Lisa, I went into the house and asked Lisa if she had been outside. She looked puzzled and said no, she said that she had been watching me running around with the washing on my own and it had made her laugh. She said I was silly and it was good to see me laugh, which just made me want to cry so much, I must have been such a shadow of a person back then.

Of course I had been through some traumatic times with Roses death and Paul leaving me. I was of course drinking rather a lot so it's easy to jump to the conclusion that it was in my head, that perhaps I had a breakdown or an 'episode'. I to be honest, I thought the same thing, but it lingered in me how could it be so vivid. How could I be so convinced that I played with Lisa in the garden? I thought that maybe it was a guilt reaction to not being there enough for Lisa, perhaps I created a fantasy to make up for the emotional neglect perhaps I was responsible for.

I went to the Doctor, I had to be careful what I told him for I didn't want to come across as an unfit parent and have Lisa taken away from me. He prescribed me some tricyclic antidepressants, which were fine in terms of coping with life, but not so fine with the weight gain, drowsiness, and constipation. It did wean me of the drink as I was so tired in the evenings, too tired to get pissed all the time. The weight gain didn't bother me at all as I never felt sexy or attractive anyway, at this time of my life, after Paul's cruel words. I felt like my only purpose was to be as good a mother as I could to Lisa. I didn't get huge, but I went from about nine stone to about twelve, I guess a positive, looking back, was that I got curvier.

One night I was in bed and I heard footsteps on the landing, little footsteps padding across the carpet. I thought it was Lisa up to use the loo, I always kept the landing light on so we could see when we woke up, also, I got a bit scared and lonely living on my own with Lisa when she was younger. I lay there and listened and I heard soft breathing outside my bedroom door. By the time I sat up the door was open and Lisa was just stood there in the doorway. I thought *is she ok? Has she had a bad dream or maybe she can't sleep?* Lisa hated thunder and lightning and she would get into bed with me if she was scared by it. I don't blame anyone for being frightened by a thunderstorm, especially if you have been asleep and it rolls close to your home, it can be quite a shock. I said something like *are you ok baby?* she just stood there, her silhouette in the door frame with light behind her and she said nothing. She stood there, breathing softly and I thought maybe she was sleepwalking, I hear it's dangerous to wake up a sleep walker, I started to gently get out of bed and she quietly said *"It's not your fault mummy, it really isn't, I'm ok, I promise."* And with that she vanished, completely vanished in a blink of an eye. I was confused to say the least and I hopped out of bed and out onto the empty landing. There was no one there, I checked the bathroom and again no one there, I checked in Lisa's room she was fast asleep in her bed.

I went back to bed and wondered what had happened, I knew I was awake, I was certain of that. I thought about the medication I was on, I thought maybe I had hallucinated, maybe I had 'tripped' on them and imagined Lisa getting up. I thought nothing more of it and went back to bed with no incident.

In the morning over breakfast I asked Lisa if she had slept O.K., she said yes and told me she'd had a lovely dream, in which her and Rose were playing hide and seek in the house last night. Lisa very rarely spoke about Rose, in the eighteen months or so since the accident, Lisa had barely spoken about her. Over the following months Lisa had many sessions with a school counsellor, but Lisa had been adamant that she was O.K. and that Rose was happy and playing with her friends in Heaven. I still have the counsellor's reports somewhere and apart from the initial period when Rose was killed Lisa had just been calm about it all. She had handled it in a very mature fashion, which psychologically can be very worrying when a child of that age is involved. They say it can create deep rooted mental and emotional issues later in life, but you can't make a child grieve can you? You cannot force them to react to it. I did talk to Lisa about it on the anniversary of Rose's death. On her ninth birthday Lisa had told off a girl in school for only putting her name on her birthday card and not her sisters. I had sat down with her and explained how the poor girl was only trying to be nice. I explained how once someone had gone to heaven, although we still thought about them and missed them and remembered the time they had on the earth with us, that people tended not to send them a card anymore. Lisa asked why that was, she said that we should still keep celebrating their birthday regardless, whether they were here or not. At the time I believed that once you were dead you were dead, but I wasn't going to tell a nine year old that, she would make her own conclusions in life and what happened next, after death. Looking back it was a very loving attitude expressed by Lisa; we should keep celebrating the dead's birthday. Some cultures do.

One night I was in bed and again I heard the soft footsteps on the landing, the door opened and there was Lisa, stood there with the light pouring in behind her. I was convinced it was Lisa and that it wasn't some strange random girl that had decided to break in. That would be ludicrous. I got out of bed this time and as I got closer to her she said *"Mummy, I've just been sat with Lisa, she's having nice dreams."* A chill went through my entire body in a wave, from the top of my scalp all the way to my feet. As I got close to the girl, I saw her face which was badly and horrifically injured. I remember the sound I made, it haunts me to this today, I made a sound like an injured animal, a sound I cannot replicate and I crashed to my knees. I was shaking uncontrollably and wet myself. I lost all control. It wasn't Lisa in front of me stood in my door way. It was Rose.

Spirituality

Judith: When something like that happens you just think you have gone insane. I can't remember much of that night; I guess I was in shock. Lisa said nothing in the morning and I said nothing about the experience. I needed time to try and understand what had happened, I needed time to work out if I had indeed had a breakdown. You ask yourself questions like *are you a fit mother?* Society happily tells us that seeing dead people is not appropriate. Such people are to be frowned upon, seen as mad or as charlatans.

For the next few days I don't think I got any sleep. I lay at the bottom of the bed with the door open, expecting to see her again. To see little rose stood there disfigured and mutilated as the day I saw her dead body for the first time. I didn't see her.

Lisa just got on with life, I felt she had a knowing about her and I just needed her to say something like *"Mum, did you see Rose last night?"* or *"I dreamt Rose was talking to us."* I needed her to say anything that would perhaps make sense of what had happened. Lisa said nothing.

About a week after the appearance of Rose I was parked at the supermarket at the top of Haverfordwest, I was returning my trolley and was in a daze still. I hadn't slept or eaten much since and I was running on fumes. I was just about to put my trolley in the bay and this very beautiful smiling young lady asked if she could have my trolley, I was almost oblivious to her and I said she could. She took the trolley from me and said *"Your little girl is sorry she scared you, she's been too scared to say hello again."*

I was taken back, angry and shocked in fact that a complete stranger had said this. Was this some practical joke? I asked the woman to explain herself, she smiled and apologised, said she did not mean offense and sometimes she forgot herself. She told me there was a little girl running around the parked cars, playing hide and seek, it was my daughter, she said that even now the girl had no fear of cars.

I was numb, I thought I would faint. The woman grabbed my arm to steady me. Her touch was warm and soft, she was so reassuring. She smiled and said that she would walk me to my car. I sat in the driver's seat with the door opened and she knelt there asking if I was O.K. I started crying, asking what this was. What was happening? I asked if I had gone completely mad, she casually replied I had not .It was a shock to me how some random woman in a supermarket car park had seen the spirit of my child. She laughed and said it was natural. She put her hands out and I held them, I wept and wept. She held me close and for the first time in years I let it all out. This woman, a complete stranger, It felt like she was an old friend, someone I could trust, someone who cared for me, like she was a person who loved me.

The beautiful woman was Rachel and that day she changed my life forever. She explained that some people have a gift. It was a true and beautiful gift to see what lies beyond the veil, that when people we love die, they don't always pass straight into the spirit world. She said my little girl wanted to be with her mummy and her sister. People can disbelieve it as hokum and nonsense but imagine how I felt , how depressed and unsure I was as a woman, as a mother, and then this beautiful soul from nowhere opens a door for me to let the light in, to help me find peace.

If any of you have lost anyone, and are riddled with grief and sadness and guilt, let go of that big sack of rocks, just drop them and embrace the notion that you can make amends, you can say goodbye. Imagine having the chance to tell someone you lost that you love them, that you still love them every day. Sometimes we lose people so suddenly, so tragically. Maybe that morning we could have been nicer, or taken more time to listen or just given them that hug or told them, simply, that you loved them. You can never tell someone enough that you love them; you may feel it's stupid or daft but tell them, let them know how amazing life is because they are in it.

Rachel taught me all of this. She was part of a local spiritual church and asked me to come along, she said she would teach me and show me. She explained I had a gift too, that it ran in the family and could be harnessed and controlled, so it did not become so confusing and frightening.

I began to attend the Church and its spiritualist service and was surrounded by many incredible people. Some who were incredibly ill and others who had lost loved ones. I saw people riddled with cancer smiling and singing and parents of dead children so thankful to hear a message from them. The mediums were so genuine and sensitive and loving. During the healing sessions you could literally feel the warmth and energy surrounding us. It was not a stuffy, bible thumping, fire and brimstone experience, but one of enlightenment, of love and hope and of faith and miracles. Anyone reading this should seek out their nearest spiritualist church and just sit in one service, you will understand then how wondrous it is.

For the first time in years I felt alive, I made friends again, I wasn't afraid to feel sexy and beautiful or to meet men. I went to conventions all over the U.K and embraced everything. I was growing. Gone was the sad grey and miserable woman, I was a bright and beautiful flower reaching out for the sun.

Over time I began to truly open up, I explored all manner of spiritual beliefs and practices and have seen and experienced many wonderful things. People are so frightened by the unknown, but once you understand it then it's not so scary. Some of the spirits look horrific from illness or injury, but if it was someone you loved, would you overlook that? Of course you would. They are still human souls at the ends of the day. There are some bad spirits that were bad people, same as there are bad living people. There are other things too, these are not human, they never were and they are terrifying. These entities wreck homes, wreck lives and feed off the negativity, the anger and the depression they wilfully cause. Heartbreak and hatred are like a drug to these entities, empowering them. I bless and cleanse homes and offer spiritual guidance to other people. All of this, thanks to that one woman in the supermarket car park who offered her love and support. She has moved away but we still keep in touch.

I spoke to Rose many times. At first I broke down and sobbed and sobbed, seeing her there so terribly injured, I soon overlooked the physical injury and just saw my beautiful girl. As Lisa grew up into a beautiful young woman, Rose remained young, she is perpetually young now.

Rose never blamed me, she said she felt no pain when she died, she just missed playing with Lisa. She said a spirit boy had told her they should go to the spirit world, but she didn't want to, not yet, she felt it wasn't her time. Rose passed on, into the spirit realm, I still have long distance communication with her, as I like to call it, and she is happy. Her face has healed, she told me, and she doesn't look so scary anymore. Bless her. She has told me a few things that were a shock, to be honest, things that I never expected. I wouldn't even know how to begin to explain what she has told me.

I love her as much as if she were alive sat in front of me now, I know that when I pass she will be there, my beautiful girl and we will be together again. She is my darling daughter, my beautiful precious girl.

Lisa started to have some serious problems with her home, a tremendous power, a huge and dark force lurked there. One day I saw what was there and it sent a chill through my soul. Lisa has no idea what is there, no idea what is happening, I am afraid with this one that not even I can help. It might not be my help she needs, there is another.

Action

The experiences that the family have shared with me have intrigued and disturbed me greatly. Never in all my years of investigation, have I ever received such detailed and continuous accounts of activity spread over three generations. I decide I have passed the point of no return and realise that secrets are being kept from me. I need all the information I can get in order to dissect these accounts into a fathomable narrative. Could it be that the family have concocted this elaborate series of hauntings, metaphysical attacks and supernatural activity, for a motive unknown to me at this time?

Their relationships seem strained as if each one is holding something back from the others. I mull over the notion that perhaps this is a hoax, that the secrets and withheld information are nothing more than smoke and mirrors, to disguise holes in their stories, perhaps leading my investigation off track.

I sit in front of Lisa, her hand holding a cigarette, her index finger yellow and stained from chain smoking. She is agitated, she is afraid, and despite my doubts I cannot but feel for her. If what she says has happened, is in fact real, then she is the victim of a terrible wrong doing. In this section I have put the accounts of all three of the family members together, in an attempt for you to understand the different perceptions regarding the spectral intrusion and I ask you to ask yourself, what would you do?

Lisa: I called Mum. I didn't want to. Not only did I feel ashamed of what had happened, but also, I just couldn't deal with her mumbo jumbo at this time. No one can tell me that it's all O.K. I don't want to hear that the spirits mean no harm. I had been sexually assaulted against my will and shaking some incense about is not going to remove the stench of the memory, the feeling of it inside me. Could you fully understand how that makes you feel? To have no power or control over what is happening to you? I feel so sad and angry for people that have been raped or sexually abused, but in their case sometimes there can be justice, sometimes there can be help. You can't handcuff a ghost and put it on trial and throw it in jail.

To the people out there reading or hearing this, however it works; I want you to imagine something inside you. I don't care if you are a man or a woman but imagine something inside you; something touching you, feeling you, thrusting inside you and you can't stop it. You can feel it inside you cold, throbbing and swelling, pushing as deep as it can inside you. Imagine if you woke up one night and there was a person on top of you having sex with you. A total stranger, you couldn't scream for help as you had been drugged, but you can still witness it and feel its unloving intrusion on you.

Judith: Lisa called me. She tried to be calm but seconds later she broke down. I couldn't understand her. She was sobbing and whimpering and my first thought was that something terrible had happened to Tyler, an accident, or he'd got into trouble with the police or something. I told her that I would be over as soon as I could. When I put the phone down, a huge chill went through me.

I got there and Lisa was sat in the living room, it was thick with cigarette smoke, I could smell sick too. She was sat there, pale and in shock. I headed over and hugged her and I thought she would break me. She wouldn't let go and I couldn't breathe. Her whole body was shaking.

Tyler: I remember that morning, Mum was acting so strange. I thought she was on drugs. She gave me something like forty quid and told me go out for the day as she wanted to clean up the house and wanted a bit of peace. I thought great and I went out with my mates.

Judith: I got Lisa to calm down, to take a deep breath and I sat her down on the settee. She looked at me and burst into a long anguished howl. I had never seen her as upset as this. I tried to make sense of what she was saying but I couldn't understand. She calmed a little, taking huge breaths, her bottom lip trembling. Eventually she lay on the settee and she just fell asleep.

Lisa: I was so exhausted that I think I just passed out with Mum there. I remember sending Tyler out. I didn't want to be on my own but I didn't want him to see me like that. I must have slept for an hour and I woke up. I was so confused to what had happened. Mum was sat in front of me and she had a big glass of water on the coffee table and a large cup of tea ready. It was like when you have been drunk and you wake up and can't remember where you are or how you got there, then like a bad dream you start to remember bits of the night and you think *oh god!*

Well take that feeling and times it by a million. I started to shake again but Mum sat by me, put her arm around me and told me to sip some water. She held me for ages, I felt like I was a child again. When you are little you have so much faith in your parents. They are supermen, wise and invincible. I needed her love and compassion so much. Mum looked me straight in the eyes and asked if I was O.K. She said that I needed to tell her what had happened. I told her.

Judith: My little girl told me that a ghost had raped her. Do you have any idea how powerless and angry that makes you feel as a parent? I never said a word; I contained my anger and distress and just held her. Showing my anger would not undo what had been done. I needed to be calm and collected for her. I needed to take control while being there for her.

She told me everything in detail; she was ashamed and guilty and started to howl again when she told me that she nearly had an orgasm. I told her she had done nothing wrong, she had no control over her body and not to blame herself or feel ashamed.

Lisa: I guess I'm lucky to have a Mother who I can tell I was sexually abused by a ghost and she didn't look at me like I was a nutter.

Judith: I told Lisa not to worry, she and Tyler could stay at mine for a few days till I could make some calls and get some help. I told Lisa to ring work and say that she was ill and would be back in a few days. I needed to speak to my friends at the church. Lisa agreed, I told her to get dressed and we would leave a note for Tyler to come over to mine.

Lisa: I knew it was no good calling the police as there was no evidence. Just the word of a woman who went out and had some drinks and next thing she's crying rape. I want you to know that I didn't want to leave my house; I didn't want it to think it had beaten me. I just needed some time to re-group, to let Mum do her thing and hopefully I could have my home back. Mum said we would see if we could get another house somewhere; see if the council had a house swap available. It broke my heart to think like that but at the time you just want to fuck off and leave all that shit behind.

Tyler: Mum was spending some time at Nan's, I asked could I just stay at home on my own but mum got cross and said I had to stay with her. It was Nan who told me what had happened. She told me that night, when Mum was asleep. Nan is pretty straight like that, she pulls no punches. She told me our house was haunted or possibly possessed by an incubus and that Mum had been sexually violated by it. At sixteen I was pretty fucking shocked and sickened to be honest. At first I thought how can Nan tell me this sick shit, but when I looked into her eyes I saw she was deathly serious, I thought about all the haunting stuff and thought maybe this was true. How would you react if you heard your Mum was raped by a demon or a ghost? Its batshit crazy, I just wanted to get a petrol bomb and burn our whole house down to the ground. I was furious beyond belief, absolutely tamping.

Nan said she had a plan and was convinced that her mates at the spiritualist church would help and they would perform some kind of exorcism. She was pretty sure they would get our home back, she said that Mum would need a lot of love and attention, that she would get over this in time but it would take a while. I guess something like that would.

Lisa: I did worry that if something had the power to do that to me, what if it turned it's attentions on Tyler. It might not only be into women, maybe it liked men too.

Maybe it would assault him. I tell you now, that some crazy things were going on in my head at that time.

Tyler: I never thought about it trying to have sex with me at the time, that's quite a frightening thought though.

Judith: Lisa stayed at mine for a few days. Tyler asked if he could just go home, he said he could look after himself but I don't think he fully realised just how powerful this entity was. It's not a question of how tough you are or how strong you are. Physical means cannot stop a spirit or a demon. You can't shoot it or hit it with a cricket bat or throw fire at it or call the police.

I spoke to some of the more experienced members in my church, they agreed that we had to keep this amongst ourselves, we could not allow this at the time to be made public. We had to keep it a secret. We could not afford for every oddball ghost hunter, no offense, or the papers, to swarm the home looking for a story. We did not want to fuel the power of the presence in the home. I hope you understand but we used our own methods to cleanse the house and I am not at liberty to tell you what those methods are. It is sacred to the people involved and something that we don't want non-believers, or those with no experience, to dabble in. Remember the door to the spirit world can be opened to, not just closed on, intruder spirits. Too many people have played with Ouija boards, séances and played at being clueless amateur ghost investigators. They have no idea how many doors they have left wide open for a multitude of spirits, and sometimes much worse, to enter our realm.

Lisa: A few days after the assault, Mum come home. She had been gone for about two days. She came in tired and frail. She came up to me and gave me the biggest hug ever and said that Tyler and I could go home. I cried so much that morning. The relief was huge. I believed in Mum and I believed in her friends at the church. They are wonderful, kind and beautiful people. I went home.

Tyler: We went home and I have to admit that it didn't feel like home. I know Nan and her friends cleansed it but all I had in my mind was Mum being abused. That's an awful image to have in your head. Can you think of your parents in that way? I think it took us both a few weeks to settle back into our home.

Lisa: Taking that first step back into my home was nerve racking. I honestly felt sick at the thought of stepping into my own house. I had this big ball of knots in my stomach but I stepped in and Mum had tidied the place, she had put flowers in vases, lit incense sticks and done us some shopping. It didn't feel the same as it had the day after the attack. It felt bright and warm and I had every faith in Mum. Well I had to, didn't I? I had to believe it was over. I would never doubt or stop believing in the supernatural, I would always be weary of what entered into our world, but Mum said she had closed the door and Tyler and I were now safe.

Judith: All I can tell you of the cleansing was that it was exhausting and at times violent. It's like when the police and council try and evict travelers or squatters. You see it on the news, it gets nasty and violent and people chain themselves to gates. They just don't want to leave and it takes a huge effort to move them. The time for talk and negotiations are over and it's time to shift them. That was what the cleansing was like. I know the Catholic Church have exorcisms but what we did that day was something different and very, very difficult but we succeeded...for a time.

Defilement

We advise due caution with this section as it contains a very violent, graphic and disturbing account that some will find difficult to read. The words used to describe the ordeal are based on the actual experiences of those involved and regardless of the validity of the occurrence the

imagery presented is one of a most unsettling nature.

Lisa: Things were good for many years, maybe two or so. I don't think anything unusual happened in the house. I was weary about the house for a while and something like that you can never forget, but as the weeks turned into months I soon began to relax and enjoy my life as I had before. The house seemed brighter and warmer.

I did some research into what had happened to me and it wasn't uncommon, there were many stories about such things and I felt for the people who had to go through it. I was tempted to maybe join or start a group so that there was support for other victims, but Pembrokeshire is a small place and I couldn't find or hear from anyone local who had experienced the same. I would imagine there are few people that would admit to being the victim of such an obscene supernatural violation. The nearest person reported to have been sexually assaulted by a suspected ghost was in Swansea, which is about an hour and half away by train. As time passed so did the need to pursue it. Mum, as far as I was concerned, had stopped what had happened and Tyler and I just moved on with our lives

Tyler: We just got on with it, there were times when I would wake up and think there was something in the house, but I think that happens to most people at some time. You are going to be paranoid after something like that happens to your Mum in your home. There were no voices or sounds in the attic, no electrical charges or orbs and I never saw or smelt the Shitty Man again during this time, as far as I knew Mum was fine and nothing happened to her. I had friends and girlfriends stay over and they never complained about it.

I wouldn't say that I was interested in the paranormal as a result of what happened but my ears would prick up whenever anyone talked about it. There was this guy I spoke to in the pub and he said that a few years back, when he was around ten or eleven, he and his twin brother had been awoken by a ghost in the night at his Aunties house. Things had been really bad there and still went on to this day but I thought, quite selfishly, at least ours had stopped. Mum wouldn't watch any horror movies or T.V shows like the *X-files* or *most haunted* as it was a part of her life she wanted to put behind her and I could understand that.

Lisa: Tyler was about eighteen or nineteen when it started again...it was soul destroying what it did to me...what Tyler had to witness. Everything I have told you so far, everything that had happened is easy compared to telling you about that night.

Tyler: When it came back, oh my God, it was fucking horrendous, it was fucking terrible. No son should have to see that happen to their own Mother and be unable to stop it. I was powerless. I will never, ever, as long as I live be able to get what happened to her that night out from my mind. I get very angry just thinking about it. I haven't spoken to anyone really about it. I've just bottled it up. I can't just talk to my Mrs or my friends casually about what happened, it weighs so heavy on me. I think in a way it is why I am talking to you now.

Sometimes when I have been intimate, you know? Having sex I get little flashbacks, like vivid memories of what happened that night. I see Mum and I see what it did to her and I don't want to finish the sex, you can't with images like that in your mind. Sex is pleasure, sex is fun, and it's about being close to someone you want to be with. What I saw was nothing at all like how it should be.

There are sick fucking people in this world. Murderers and rapists and child molesters and that thing should go after them, not her. What the fuck has she ever done to anyone? She's been a good woman and she has done without to look after me, to be kind to other people. She's been shit on by men yet she keeps going on with a smile and works hard. I love my Mum so much but it took a while to see her in the same way, to see her as my Mum. I don't know what I thought of her and it wasn't even her fault yet I judged her. I was ashamed as no child should have to see their parent like that, never. We all joke about seeing our parents shagging or hearing the bed squeaking but this isn't like that at all, this was torment and torture and for a minute I wanted to abandon her and run off and never see her ever again. I wished it wasn't real.

Lisa: Where do I begin? I remember the night as if it was last night. You never forget something like that and if you think the first assault was bad then this is a billion times worse. I have been so worried about telling this part for so long. It has kept me up at night from the time we first made contact to do the interviews. I chain smoke just running through it in my mind; I worry about how much detail I give to you. I worry that I won't explain it properly or that if I say a word out of place then People will think I made it all up.

People out there can think what they want and I'm sorry if they think this is shit, that this is a great big lie to make money or for any other gain. I don't want anything but to get this off my chest, to maybe hear from others who have had similar experiences. Maybe I can help them; maybe we can help each other. If I am the only person in the world that this has happened to then so be it. I wouldn't wish this on anyone. You have no idea how grim this is, how disgusting and sick I feel by just sitting here thinking about the words I am going to use and about what I am about to say. If people out there are getting a thrill or think it's all about ghosts having sex then I'm sorry, nothing will prepare you for what I'm about to say. I know I sound really angry but I know what people are like and I just want them to understand how much this affected me, how much it affected my own flesh and blood and how it keeps on affecting me years after. To this day that night lingers in my mind and I pray nobody and I mean nobody has had to endure anything like it. People can think I'm mad or on drugs, they really can and I wish I was on something sometimes just to suppress the memory. This is what happened.

It was a Friday night; I had finished work and was settling down on the couch to watch some T.V. I wasn't with anyone at the time and Tyler was in his late teens. I think he had been working nights at a supermarket in Haverfordwest that week, he had a weekend off and was out on the beer. It was about ten, maybe a bit later, I had a bath, put on my dressing gown and made myself a tea. I can't remember what was on T.V; I think I was watching a film on Film 4. Not sure.

About midnight I started to doze and I thought *time for bed.* I was so tired and I had to will myself off the settee; I could have easily dropped off there. I often wondered what would have happened if I had stayed downstairs. It's silly thinking like that, as sometimes I think *it is what it is*, something as rotten and powerful as this, would have gotten me no matter what.

I went up to bed and for a split second felt all my hairs on my arms rise and felt a tingling on my scalp all the way down my back. It was freezing cold but it passed. I won't lie to you, I did think *is it back?* But it happened and passed quickly, so I thought nothing more of it and went into my room. I took off my dressing gown, I had my knickers and bra on underneath and I was so tired that I just got in to bed like that. I must have fallen asleep as soon as my head hit the pillow.

Tyler: I had been out to a few pubs in the Dock and I think I'd had a row with the girl I was seeing. You know? The stupid rows you have when you're pissed. I will admit now to you, I was steaming. I had drunk a lot that night. I was tired when I got out from working nights all week, I didn't eat much and had just been paid so went a little crazy on the larger and shorts. I must have been out drinking for about five hours, maybe more. The boys were getting a taxi into Haverfordwest to go to some of the clubs there, to go on the pull, but I wasn't in the mood after the falling out. I went home; I staggered home to be honest. I got there and it took me ages to open the door, to get the key in. As soon as I opened the door there was this terrible smell, really fucking bad, like someone had shit in the hall way. I thought maybe I had stepped in dog shit.

I checked my shoes, I think I actually fell over checking them and then I heard this knocking upstairs and a weird moaning noise. I thought that maybe mum had a man in her life who she had kept secret from me and was shagging up there. I tried to be quiet and I stumbled into the kitchen. I put on the kitchen light and the smell was awful, it was so sickly that I thought I was going to be sick. I think I grabbed a beer from the fridge, grabbed a few bags of crisps, I made it into the living room and put on the T.V. I just lay on the settee.

I sat there in the dark, apart from the light of the T.V., the noise upstairs was getting louder and the smell was getting worse. I remember opening the window to let some air in. That is how bad the smell was. The knocking and this weird moaning noise just kept getting louder and quicker, I will be honest that it's not what you want to hear is it? You don't want to hear your Mum having sex, especially noisy rampant sex. I didn't mind as she probably didn't know I was home or thought that maybe I would have stayed at the Mrs'. I have had sex in my room with girls and I always try to be quiet as its embarrassing isn't it? You don't want your mum to catch or hear you shagging, do you?

I think I'd been home for about half an hour when I heard this scream and then a shout for help. It came from upstairs and I thought *what the fuck is happening?* I didn't know if I should leave her or go up. I thought I better go and check, I thought if I make a load of noise that maybe she would hear me and stop what she was doing. I went into the hallway and I opened and closed the front door really loudly and shouted *"Hello"* like I had just come in. The stench in the hallway was terrible. I started to climb the stairs with a noisy footstep on each just so she knew I was home and with each step the smell got worse and the knocking and moaning got louder. By the time I got to the top of the stairs I had to cover my nose and mouth with the sleeve of my jacket. It was the worst smell ever.

I called out *"Mum, you ok?"* and from her room I heard a pitiful sob of *"Tyler, please help."* I opened Mums bedroom door and it was dark. It was stinking in there, worse than anywhere else in the house, I flicked on the light and I was appalled. It was fucking sickening.

Lisa: I am ashamed that my son had to see me like that; I am disgusted that my own son had to see what he had. It's wrong, so very wrong.

Tyler: What I saw, what I witnessed, I pray that none of you ever, and I mean ever, have to see something like that.

When the light went on the first thing I saw was Mum on all fours facing the wall. Her backside was facing me; she was naked apart from her bra. There was shit all down her legs and her buttocks were opening and closing like someone was spreading and closing them. I could see her anus gaping open with blood and shit dribbling from it. I was sick, I actually vomited, and I was shocked and disgusted. I couldn't see Mums face but she was making this weird moaning sound, her hair was hanging over her face and her arm was behind her back like something was holding it.

I didn't know what to do; nothing can prepare you for that. It looked like something was having sex with her anus, but there was no one there, her buttocks were moving and her anus was stretched open. I just freaked, I ran to grab her and I was forcefully pushed back against the wall. I was frozen. I couldn't move. I was frozen stiff, powerless and paralyzed and I vomited again all over myself.

Then Mum's whole body started to move, like rotate to the left a little. It was almost as if she was levitated a few inch's and then she just faced me. Her hair matted and covered in sick and her mouth was making this weird moaning sound, not of pleasure, no way, this was one of pain and agony.

It seemed forever that I watched her. I think I was sick again and I saw bile drooling from her mouth. I couldn't move or scream and it was like whatever was doing this wanted to watch me, having to see my own mother being abused and raped like that by something invisible and evil.

Lisa: As I said, my head hit the Pillow as soon as I got to bed, and as far as I knew I had fallen asleep. Then next thing I'm on all fours and something is inside me, inside my arse, I cannot move, I cannot call out. There is an awful smell of diarrhea in the room.

I started to cry and I started to think, *not again, why is this happening again?* But this was not like before, when it was kissing my breasts and trying to pleasure me, no, this was worse, this was brutal and it buggered me for what seemed like hours. I think I passed out with the pain and the fear. I could feel something long and scaly or like sand paper deep inside me. It was thrusting and tearing. It was agonizing; it was penetrating me so deep. It never touched my vagina or my chest or my mouth. All its focus was on my anus and buttocks.

I have never had anal sex before and the pain was insane. I felt like my anus was burning and ripping, I could feel blood dripping down my legs, I think I shit myself a few times too, I was certainly sick all over myself and the bed. Whatever this was it left me with no dignity; it treated me like a lump of meat, like an animal. The pain was so excruciating that I thought I would die the longer it carried on. I did pray to God that he would just take me, to just let me die rather than for this to continue any longer.

I think I passed out, when I came too It was still violating me. It was awful, I heard the front door and somehow managed to scream out. It took every ounce of my power, I was so weak yet I managed to call out and next thing Tyler is in the room. Whatever had hold of me spun me around and I saw Tyler and his face, his poor face more than anything, is what hurts me the most. His face was contorted in disgust and horror. There was his mum naked, exposed and being anally raped. He looked like he was pinned to the wall and then he was sick all over himself. I'm not sure if that was because of what he was seeing or because of the awful hellish smell. He closed his eyes, I felt like he had abandoned me, left me to my torture that he had zoned out to a safer place, but who could blame him?

Then it was like as if something else came into the room, something different.

Tyler: I was there trapped against the wall, unable to move. I will be honest in that I did close my eyes, I could not bear to see my Mum like that, being brutalized, covered in her own sick and shit. I just wanted to run, to leave her there and run as fast as I could down the street and not look back. I feel so bad about saying that now but I remember just wanting to run away at that moment. I'm just being honest. Suddenly there was this strange noise. It was like electricity in the air, I remember all the hairs on my body standing up. The room was filling up with what seemed to be an electrical charge, I opened my eyes and the bedroom light began flickering.

I saw what appeared to be a bluish ball of light appear, like an orb, from the corner of the room and it shot into an area slightly above Mum, the light went out and I just heard mum coughing and sobbing. I fell to the bedroom floor in a heap just hoping and praying that it was over. No one can ever imagine, unless they had been there, how terrifying and disturbing it was. My poor mum degraded like that.

Lisa: I remember this feeling, like the room was beginning to charge with electricity and I felt the thing inside me feel less intrusive, almost as if it was melting. Then the light went out, I just collapsed into the bed and whatever had been inside me had gone. I didn't feel the rough hand of something on my arse. All I could feel was the pain in my anus and in my stomach. I lay there panting and sobbing. Tyler didn't come to me for what seemed an age; I think he was in shock. I don't think he knew how to cope, how to react. I just lay there in my own shit and vomit. One thing I did notice was that the overpowering smell vanished, it was just the awful smells that had come from us. Tyler was covered in vomit.

I felt so ashamed, so violated and the pain was so incredible but I was relieved for it to be over. I tried to crawl over to Tyler, I felt someone grab me and hold me and I thought, *no, not again* but it was -Tyler holding me and crying into my hair. It didn't matter what had happened, it didn't matter that my son had seen his mum have to endure a forced anal entry, he just loved me and he held me. I cried for an eternity.

Tyler: I held mum for ages. I felt guilty for just wanting to run off and leave her. I felt so ashamed and I just held her. I cried and cried. We both did. I didn't care what I had seen or how she looked, she was my mum and there in the dark I held her and she just shook and sobbed beneath me. Whatever was doing this had no regard for her, it wanted to hurt her and I wanted to hurt it. I would have smashed it to bits if I could have. I was puzzled by the energy in the room that appeared just before it stopped hurting Mum. It was almost as if something else was in there with us, like something helped her.

We lay for ages and then I smelt the shitty smell again, so strong, so suffocating and I thought it's come back for Mum, we shouldn't have stayed here, we should have ran out on the street and screamed for help. Mum was panting underneath me and she held me tight, she knew whatever it was, was coming back for her and she knew there was nothing I could do to stop it.

Lisa: The smell came back and I thought it was going to violate me again. There was no way on earth I could have endured that again. The Bedroom door was open from when Tyler barged in and it was dark on the landing. I think the power to the whole house was off, Tyler told me later that he left the kitchen light and T.V on when he came upstairs but there was no sound or light from downstairs. The terrible smell was creeping back into the room, as I peered through my fingers I saw a blue flash on the landing, I thought I could hear muffled voices arguing and shouting but in a weird hushed way. There was another flash and I distinctly heard a voice shout *"DO NOT TOUCH HER!"* then the smell vanished again and the light came back in the bedroom.

Tyler: It was like the time I heard the voices from the attic, like two men shouting but in a whispering kind of way. A voice demanded that *it leave her alone* and the smell went and the lights came back on and I could hear the T.V on downstairs. It was about 2 a.m. I managed to get Mum to sit up, I asked her if she wanted me to call the police or anybody and she said no, she asked that I just help her to the bathroom. She could barely stand and it took a while to get her to the bathroom. She sat on the toilet sobbing but she asked that I put the shower on. She got in and just held herself crying as the shit and blood washed off her. It was such a terrible sad sight to see mum sat there, broken and abused. Mum is such a good, kind, loving woman and she didn't deserve that, no one does.

I asked her again if I should call the police and she whispered in a frail voice that they wouldn't believe us and they might accuse me of raping my own mum, which did make me furious but I guess she was right. There was no one else in the house but me and it was obvious that she was the victim of a sexual assault. I would be a suspect and in a small town like Pembroke Dock, regardless if I was innocent or not, I would be ruined for life and forced to move away.

I asked her if she wanted me to call Nan but she gave me a cold hard stare and gently shook her head. She asked that I get her some painkillers and her tampons and said she would patch herself up, She said I should go and stay at my girlfriends for a bit while she tried to get us a new home but I refused saying I wouldn't leave her. I said we would get through this together.

Mum asked that I grab everything in the bedroom and put them in the washing machine and then put them in bin bags and bin them. I told her again it was evidence and we should at least take pictures, she quietly said no and began sobbing again. I left her there under the water while I stripped the bed, pulled up the rug in there and took her dressing gown downstairs. They were stinking but not as bad as the smell that had filled the house. I thought we would need a fumigator but a day later there was no smell, there was no evidence of what had happened just the memories etched in our mind. Mum had more physical pain and she had to use tampons on her behind for weeks until she was fully healed. Every time she went to the toilet, she would nearly pass out with the pain. She stopped eating and took Imodium for nearly a week. I wanted her to go to the doctors and just say she'd had rough anal sex with a partner but she refused. She was stubborn. She had to take weeks off work, she refused to speak to Nan, when she asked the council if we could move they said there was nothing available, we didn't have enough money to go and live somewhere else.

Lisa: I remember, sat there in the shower with the water covering me. that we couldn't get any help from anyone.

What would you do if your neighbour or friend ran into your house with a bleeding and torn anus, covered in sick and shit saying they had been raped by a ghost? People may say I should have called the police, but who could it have been? Who is the suspect? Would they simply believe it was a ghost? Yes officer I was anally abused by a ghost, do you think you'll catch him? It sounds like a load of fucking nonsense and the only witness was my son. What if they charged him with sexually assaulting his own mother? Then I thought, what if they accused me of doing it to myself? How degrading and how humiliating would that be?

I was furious with Mum, she told me the house was cleansed, she told me it was safe to go home and it had been for years so why now had it come back? What was this terrible ghost's infatuation with me? and why had it been gentler the first time? and why had it been so fucking violent and degrading the second time? What had happened on the landing? Who were the voices? and what was the blue light? Then it all clicked. An epiphany I think they call it and it all made sense. I hadn't been sexually assaulted by a spirit. I had been sexually assaulted by two.

Aftermath

I am a thirty eight year old investigator of the Paranormal and have investigated the metaphysical since I was eleven. I have experienced many strange and unconventional elements associated with the study and investigation of the subject and never have I been so physically sickened and disturbed by such an account.

This is not your usual supermarket tabloid style magazine story of 'I had sex with a Ghost!' This is something far more malevolent and sinister. What concerns me is this insidious and degrading act cannot be deemed sexual as it is more of a torture and humiliation, it is a contravention of deep rooted physical, emotional and mental torture. There is no sexual gratification in its act. It is a statement from a powerful and violating entity that it can do what it wishes, has no regard for feelings or consideration of the suffering and anguish it causes to its victim.

This entity has such little regard for the lives of humans. What Lisa has had to endure is shocking beyond belief. This creature made the callous decision to face her toward her dismayed and anguished son during the maltreatment, whom by his own admission was powerless to intervene, to protect his matriarch, the woman that brought him into this world.

As I asked in *A most haunted house* what are the motives behind such un-earthly life forms? It is incomprehensible as a human, to even begin to understand the thoughts and design of these creatures, which breach our reality and do as they please. Are they after a withdrawal or surrender from our mind and souls so they can pick us off after our last breath? Are they simply wearing us down, making us weak so they can torture us further in the afterlife? There are many theories on why these entities do what they do, however, we will not know the answers until we take our final precious breath and journey into the unknown country that is death.

The forces that thrive on evil, that thrive on abuse and harm, cannot be fathomed by good willed, kind and loving people. If we were question the motives of a child, who was pulling off the wings of a fly, would they understand the suffering they were causing? Do these creatures visiting our realm have an emotional detachment towards us or possibly no emotions at all?

Are we so low on the totem pole of existence that supernatural presences regard us as we would a flea nibbling at our ankles? Do they find amusement and pleasure in the ungodliness they preside over us or do they operate on a spectrum truly beyond the scope of human rationale? Shall we ever understand their predilection with humanity?

In my shock and horror at the families account I also have to ask myself *what if they have made this up?* What twisted and immoral mind would create such a wrong doing? Several times Lisa broke down and cried in her recanting and Tyler's body language was one of fury, resentment, a man who wanted to avenge his mother's abuser. There is viciousness, a poison in his voice when he refers to the Shitty man. I still believe that Tyler is holding something back from me. I will let him replace his vitriol with calmness before I broach the subject with him again, but I will get my answer.

I look at Lisa with different eyes. If what she tells me did happen or she believes happened then she is a very brave woman. Her stubbornness is ferocious as she recants the tale in the home in which the violation took place. She explains how there was no help for her to move home, she could not ask for help from the authorities and her relationship with her mother suffered greatly as a repercussion of the assault. She had no choice but to keep living, to keep going.

I ask Lisa if she needs a break but she feels compelled to push on, she tells me that she needs to tell this, her testimonial is her cantharis, it is part of the healing process which she has been unable to do for so long.

Besides, I am intrigued by the notion that there were two spirits in her home and what their relationship was to each other. Did Lisa in fact have a guardian angel protecting her?

Lisa: That was so hard to tell you. I know you will speak to Tyler too to get his version. It's sickening; I hate the fact that he has to tell you. I hate the fact he saw me like that. I had no dignity; I was humiliated and degraded in front of my own son.

The days and weeks that followed the attack, I call it an attack as what else can you call it? Anyway, after the attack I slept in Tyler's room. For the first week or so he stayed in there too and slept on the settee he had in there but I think he started to feel a bit suffocated by me and needed his own space. He was a young man after all and we couldn't share a bedroom for the rest of our lives, things were weird enough as they were. We were aware of nothing happening in the house, nothing unusual like the smells or the change in temperatures or electrical orbs and lights, nothing like that. Tyler suggested we move rooms, that he strip mine and move into there, we re-decorate his and I move into it. It was a good idea, I don't think I could ever have slept in that room again. To me it still reeked of the thing that raped me, even though the room had been cleaned a dozen times that first week.

The immediate days after, I was in a state of shock. I didn't tell Mum, I didn't want anything to do with her after she lied about the house being safe. I was in so much pain, physically and emotionally. No one should have to endure anything like that.

I contacted the council and asked for a house swap but they had nothing immediate. I would have taken anything as long as it was a roof over our heads but I started to think *what if it wasn't the house, what if the Ghost was following me?* I couldn't be sure that it was the house. In most films and books the haunting seems to focus on a particular house, but now and again the ghosts follow the people and I was scared of that. I don't think at that time I could have coped with the idea of these things getting me regardless of where I was.

I was tempted to get counselling, you know, for sexual abuse. But how could I pretend to be talking about another human being when there wasn't one. How could I listen to advice from a counsellor, or speak to the police or doctors when there was no proof but the injuries I had around my rectum? There was nobody to accuse or to identify.

I read pamphlets and books about rape victims and in a way it helped, but it just wasn't the same; there could be no justice or a conclusion to this. No one could ever be tried for the crime. As far as knew this thing, this dirty scunt*, would have its way with me until my dying day. One night I called the Samaritans and I told them my account, what I told you, but instead of a ghost I changed it to a man. I was so angry; I started crying and hung up. I actually feel sorry for the poor person on the other end of the phone.

I was in a lot of pain inside too, it had penetrated deep, deep inside me. It was an agony that I had never experienced before. As I said I have not had anal sex before, it has never appealed to me. Even though Ian was a clumsy lover, he was young, he never hurt me on purpose. Then there was Leon, Leon was very passionate but gentle and loving.

I know women in work who say they have anal sex when they're on their period or when they have had a few beers but I never fancied it. What that thing did to me, it damaged and hurt me. I bled for about a week, going to the toilet left me in tears, I took so much Imodium to try and stop the pain. At night sleep hardly came at all, I was constantly on edge thinking it would come back and get me again. Tyler had an idea to keep the bedroom windows wide open so if it did happen maybe someone would hear my screaming and call the police.

Tyler was smart though as after he said to keep the windows open he got me an alarm, like a rape alarm so if anything happened again I could press it and someone would hear and come rescue me. We lived at the end of a street with two old people adjoining our house but it was worth a try, even if it gave me some small comfort. I would sleep with my back pressed tight against the wall and obviously I was fully dressed in bed, stupid things like having belts and straps on me so my clothes wouldn't come off easily and I would call for Tyler if I had to use the loo in the night. Whenever I had a shower, Tyler would sit on the landing just in case something happened. He is such a good son.

When you think about it, what can you actually do? Lock the door? Install a burglar alarm? Get a Gun, a knife or a baseball bat? You can't stop anything like that. It has a power that we can't understand and if it chooses to violate you then it will, no matter where you are or who you are with.

Tyler got a video camera and set in up in my old bedroom, he said if we could capture anything at all then maybe we could get help or move. I'm not sure how that would work but it seemed to keep him calm and occupied.

Things were difficult between us for a while, I think what he saw affected him more than anybody could ever understand. I ask now, would you like to see your parent, no matter how old they are, in that position? How would you get that image of them, abused and maltreated, from your mind? How could you just sit there and have a cuppa or supper or chat about what was happening on the soaps after that? How can you act like nothing ever happened?

One thing that did crop up in my mind, and was one of the few things to give me comfort, was whether something else intervened. Did something else, something different from the shitty man, come and save me. Tyler and I talked about it that week and he said it was as if two of these ghosts, spirits, whatever you want to call them were fighting over me. He said he had heard them arguing when he was younger. He thought that maybe there were two. One we knew as the Shitty man and the other he called the Cold sad man. He thought that the Cold sad man was the one that lingered in the house and sang the sad songs and played the music in the attic and that he roamed the house alone and miserable wanting attention.

He told me about the day when he was little, he said he had seen the shitty man sat at the top of the stairs but Nan had told him not to mention it again. I started to think, was it Shitty man who put his fingers in me the first time? Or was it the cold man? There was no bad smell and no feeling of cold. Cold man, I was sure, was the one that assaulted me the first time, it was different; he was trying to please me, not hurt me. Although I know that wouldn't make any difference, both were as wrong as each other in what they did to me. Some people out there might think I would rather the cold man try and have sex with me than the shitty man, but both felt as wrong as each other. But I can see where their thoughts are coming from, if I had to choose then I know which one is less disgusting.

The passing of time does make life easier but you always have an edge, a feeling that you can never let your guard down. A year or two passed again and nothing happened. I began to believe that maybe the Cold man got rid of the shitty man once and for all. I did some research and looked into ghosts, spirits and demonology. Even if you think you know what it is or think you know the answers, there is still no deterrent is there?

My research didn't give me anything concrete to work with. I read about the case which the film *The Entity* was based on. Some said the film wasn't based on a true story at all but I still read a book where the scientists claimed to have captured strange ghost lights hovering around her. If it was true then I felt for the woman and her family but it's not a 'my cats blacker than your cat', competition. I felt I had experienced far worse with the shitty man's attack and I knew, without a shadow of a doubt, that what happened to me was real. Tyler witnessed it too. There was someone else as well but we will get to that in a minute.

I did some research and looked into the house and the land it was built on and there was nothing to be concerned about. There was nothing obvious like a graveyard or a prison, you know, somewhere where bad things happened. There had only been fields and woodlands as far as I could tell. I hoped to find some clue, but there was nothing to hook onto. I hope that you can find something out during your investigation.

I got on with Life. I just had too. Tyler was fine, work was fine and Life got easier, I even went out with some friends one Saturday. Whenever I went out for a few drinks I would always stay at a friend's. I never wanted to be vulnerable in the house again. Tyler was still living at home at the time, I think, but he was spending more and more time with a girl he was seeing. I got on with my life, nothing seemed to be happening but I was taking no chances. You start to make connections in your head, almost like a superstition. You think well, it was a Friday night... I was drunk... I did this and I did that, so you try and avoid those situations at all cost and pray it doesn't happen again.

Anyway, I was out one night in Haverfordwest and we were at a club, I felt a little old as everyone was much younger than us lot. This guy came up and he was dancing around us and trying it on with my friend, flirting, trying to get her to dance with him, you know? I have to say, his dancing was the worst I have ever seen in my life, at one stage he was doing the running man, and somehow managed to knock over a girl walking past who was carrying about three pints, then he tried to spin around on his back like a dying turtle. It was hilarious! Then this youngish tall guy walks over and says to me "That's Kev, he thinks he's MC Hammer when he's had a few drinks. I can't dance at all, thankfully, but I can buy you a drink?" This guy seemed really charming and introduced himself as Dan. He was such a nice guy, he seemed genuinely interested in me and wasn't a letch like some of the guys you see out. I was troubled as to why he liked me, my confidence was low by this point in my life and I worried why he chose to talk to me all night but I just enjoyed his company so much. He only had eyes for me and didn't wander off to talk to other girls or check his phone every five seconds. I was worried he might be married, there's nothing worse than liking a guy and it turns out he's taken his ring off for the night.

He took me home that night and was such a gentleman, he didn't try it on or take advantage and he was so complimentary to me. We sat on his settee talking, smoking and listened to music. It was lovely and the next thing the sun was up and the birds were singing outside. I was at least ten years older than him, he was a good looking lad and he treated me so well. He asked if I fancied a drive and maybe breakfast. It was a great day and I forgot about everything that had happened with the house and the assaults.

I felt wanted and safe again but I wasn't going to push my luck, I didn't want to appear needy. Being with him felt too good to be true but that evening, I let go of my worries and fears and we had sex. I'll admit I was weary of sex; I was worried he would be rough and demanding but he was sensual and caring. There were times when I would have a flashback of the nights I was abused and start to feel anxious but he didn't ask anything of me, he was gentle and I relaxed and enjoyed it. He gave me his full attention and as I lay in bed, wrapped up in arms, satisfied, I felt a warmth and compassion that I had not felt in such a long time.

Dan was a good man; he had a good job and worked hard. He made an effort with Tyler despite only being five years older than him and Tyler did get on with him too. He never gave me any concerns or reasons to doubt him. I trusted him. He was funny and generous and couldn't do enough for me. We would have the odd row but cooler heads would prevail and he was always there for me with a hug and smile. He was... I mean, He *is* a good man.

We were together for quite some time and it was good, really good. He loved me, he showed it to me in every conceivable way but what I did...I mean, what *we* did...is unforgivable. I can't blame him for the way he feels, I don't blame him for hating me and no one, and I mean no one, can ever understand what happened to him. I can't even begin to imagine the hurt he feels. I'm a terrible person, a slut, slag, whatever you want to call me for what I did to him. I cheated on a good man; I cheated on a man who cared for me no matter what...I cheated on him with a Ghost.

Dan

I have to admit, from the words used by Lisa, that Dan would not be a willing subject for an interview to shed further light on this investigation. Lisa spoke about him with a shameful and remorseful tone; she felt her alleged treachery had hurt him in a profound manner, she truly broke the man's heart. Her words were marinated in the melancholic words of a doomed romance.

I telephoned a number given to me by Lisa, a polite and softly spoken man answered. I cautiously introduced myself to him. He seemed reserved and hesitant but was not rude to me. He asked who had given me his number and I dutifully told him the truth. To deliberately conceal my intentions from this man would be a terrible mistake. I had to be open and genuine with him regarding my motives. Transparency would gain the opportunity to find out more of this case from an outsider, someone from out of Lisa's inner circle that no longer had any ties or allegiances to the family

He took a deep breath and there was a long silence. This was better than being hung up on, at least I knew he was thinking about it. He asked what was in it for Lisa. I explained there was no monetary gain, just for her to tell a story that for all we knew maybe affecting people all over the world, people afraid, ashamed and confused by their ordeal. Then he began to cry, to sob down the phone. I listened in silence, my heart telling me to suggest I call back when he is more composed, but part of me, the investigator, hung on.

This was a man who had a deep emotional hurt and to openly display it as such, to a complete stranger on the phone, intrigued me. This was not the charming and confident man that Lisa had described; this man seemed unsure and broken. Was this due to the severance of the emotional umbilical to Lisa or was there something more? I needed to talk to him. He stopped sobbing and I gave him my assurances that his identity would remain secret, he would remain anonymous and if he still had an attachment for Lisa then this would be his chance to help her story to be told. He left me wanting more.

There was a log interminable silence and he quietly agreed. He agreed that he would talk to me, not today, but at a later date. I would have to provide signed documentation, not just from me but from Lisa also, to keep his identity secret. It was agreed and the investigation was to embark on a new path. I was now able to speak to someone other than Tyler who witnessed the paranormal transgressions bestowed upon Lisa.

I met with Dan at a coffee shop on the riverside of Haverfordwest. I sat there anxiously awaiting his arrival. He was late and I began to doubt whether he would turn up, maybe he had second thoughts. Then he arrived. I imagined Dan was a tall man, confident, tanned, immaculate, but I was greeted with a man with round shoulders, almost hunched as if he was trying to remain inconspicuous, ashamed of his height. He had grey hair and crow's feet around tired bloodshot eyes, he looked nothing like a man approaching thirty should look like. He was shabby and shuffled when we walked. He looked like a man who had surrendered his pride and esteem some time ago. This was a man who had lost interest in love and relationships.

He sat down nervously; he looked around as if he was expecting to see an unfriendly face, to attract unwelcomed attention. He was pre-occupied with the notion of being discovered talking to me. Anonymity is almost like an addiction for him. I asked him if he wanted a coffee or tea and he said no, he stated, sensibly, that he wanted to see the signed documents before we were to proceed. I produced them, he milled over them, studying each word in depth. Satisfied he looked at me and said he was happy to talk, but not here, not in public where there was the risk of eavesdropping. He recommended we walk to a quiet spot up the river. We sat on a bench overlooking the River Cleddau on a warm and sunny May morning. Satisfied we were alone and after some small talk he began to tell his account. Edited.

Dan:

Daniel: It is sad to think of what could have been, how life would have gone if things had been different. I think we take so much for granted. When something is good we don't value it enough or appreciate it enough. Maybe some people do and I was really happy, I mean really happy and you have these daydreams, these fantasies about being with someone for the rest of your life, till your dying day. I guess you should just take it one day at a time, not that it would matter with what happened with her. I admit I was a romantic and I would have been happy to have settled, maybe got married. She didn't want kids, she was in her mid-thirties then and she said as much as she loved her son she didn't want to go through the nappy changing, not going to work and not sleeping at night again. She had done all that and just wanted a quiet life. I think in hindsight she just didn't want to have a baby in the house or around her. Maybe she feared something terrible would happen to it if she did. It's not worth thinking about.

The fact that she didn't want kids didn't bother me at all, I was just happy being with her. I didn't feel the need to have a son or daughter or a legacy. I just imagined us together, on holidays, snuggled up in bed, watching T.V together. There would be no responsibilities just us together. Having fun and being happy. Some of the lads I know always say I'm a big softie and I should just shag 'em and bag 'em or fuck 'em and chuck 'em. I'm not like that at all; it is not about how many times I can get laid but how happy I can be with someone.

Now I can't be bothered with any kind of relationship at all. I just don't want anyone. I would rather be alone for the rest of my life. Before all of this I was confident in my own way and I had girlfriends, even got engaged once but it never worked out. I didn't really care too much, I just thought there is someone out there for everybody and sooner or later you meet the right one and settle down and then I met Lisa.

I know men who have been cheated on. Some are crushed and destroyed, some angry and others see it as an excuse to just get on with it and enjoy single life again. No man can understand how I feel. It's not like I came home one day and there was some guy fucking her on the bed or discovering a text or catching her out when she's been lying. At least with those situations you can confront someone, question them or look for a resolution. You can ask what was lacking. Was it me? Was it the sex? The way I look or did they just get bored? Did I not stimulate them enough? or did I not pay them enough attention? Could I have been more appreciative or loving? Maybe it's that you didn't respect them, didn't encourage them to grow and enjoy life. Whatever the answer is there is always a reason to stem back too. You can always find a cause. I just think if you are so miserable that you feel the need to have an affair then you should just put a bullet in the head of the relationship. I don't think it's fair, I think it's selfish and cowardly but then I guess every situation is different. It is such a mind fuck figuring out what happened to Lisa and me. I think I did the right thing, how can you knowingly share a bed with someone you love who is sleeping with someone else?

My mate from work discovered his girlfriend, who he was living with, was cheating on him. He told me this just before Lisa and I got together and I said he must have been raving, he must have been livid. I remember him looking at me with calm and knowing eyes and saying it wasn't her fault. It was his. He said he drank too much got wrapped up in his own insecurities and the pressures of work and a mortgage and he just fell into a self-made abyss of depression. He blamed himself and held no grudge against her at all now and wished her every happiness in the world. It's mad as that conversation started with him talking about ghosts.

I wish I could blame myself or someone else but it really isn't like that at all. Since the day I walked out over two years ago I have not slept with anyone, kissed anyone or even flirted with a girl by text or anything. I only keep in contact with my Mum and sister, they nag me to move on and settle down but they have no idea what happened. I was emotionally and mentally castrated and I can never take the chance of falling for someone again. I never want to take the risk of it happening again.

I saw things that I can't explain; I experienced things which frightened me so much that sometimes I can't sleep at night. I left my old job so I work nights now and sleep in the day. You have no idea what it's like to see what I saw. People like you and people that read your investigations think it's a bit of fun to have a scare or a fright. They may kid themselves and say it's not real or they hear a few knocks in the night and suddenly it's time to call Ghostbusters. It's not like that at all, it's fucking terrifying. Imagine a burglar or a rapist in your house. Imagine reading this and then you hear a smash downstairs and you hear someone in your house. Are you laughing now? Is it fun and games. Maybe you'll be fine; maybe the police come in time. Maybe you have a big dog or a weapon but your home is being intruded. You are being threatened. There is something in your home that wants to hurt you or take from you. How does that make you feel? Does it make you feel vulnerable? Imagine that and then think it doesn't matter if you call the police, or have a weapon or how fucking big your dog is because the thing in your home shouldn't even exist. Science can't prove it so it can't exist so you can't get any help. Yet billions of us believe in Gods we never see and we all sit around with popcorn watching horror movies and thinking this is not real and having a good time. It is real! It fucking is and it's not a good fucking time!

What I want people to really understand is how these things are in your home and they are doing things to you, to people you care about. There is no happy ending. There is no secret and magical way to get rid of them. They keep coming and coming and they wreck lives. They ruin everything.

I didn't particularly want to talk to you about this. I don't want to rehash the memory of it, but if it helps Lisa then I guess I will. Why do I want to help her? What is happening to her is not right in any way humanly possible. Maybe there is help out there. I don't know how that would be though. When you called me it all came flooding back in a huge wave of sadness and anger that I had hoped was over. I get so tired and emotional and it is hard for me to make sense of it all. I can't blame her, I shouldn't blame her. How can you still have feelings for someone who is doing what they are doing? Part of me wishes I had never met her that night. You can't turn back the clock but if there was a way then I would.

Back then I was so different. I had a great job which I was good at. I worked Monday to Friday, nine to five and rented a small flat up by the castle in Haverfordwest. It was good. Friday after work I would pop out for a few pints with the boys from work. Saturday, I would nip into town, do some shopping, pop into the bookies and put a few bets on the football, maybe nip into the pubs on castle square for a pint or two, pop home watch some football and then get ready and go out. I look back and think how golden life was back then. Ignorance is indeed bliss when the only thing you have to worry about is who Man United are playing and what shirt to wear out.

You don't ever imagine that some day you will be too frightened to go to sleep.

I remember that night. I went out with some of my mates. Kev was there, he was a nutter. He got thrown out of another place for doing the thriller dance on the bar. The bouncers were raving with him. I don't think he was even that drunk by then. The man just loved to dance. It was because of him that I met Lisa. We were in this club and we were dancing around a group of women, just being a fanny. I have to say that I didn't find any of these women particularly attractive but then I saw one and she was so beautiful. She had sullenness to her but not in an angry or miserable way. It was just something in her eyes. I introduced myself. We talked and we got on really well. I learned that Lisa was older than me, she had a son and was single. I liked her. I fancied her so much. She was easy to get on with and not full of herself like some of the younger girls I'd see out. At the end of the night I asked if she fancied doing something next weekend, maybe we could hook up again. I waited with her and her mates at the Castle Square, we were waiting for taxis and we just chatted away, Kev was steaming and was snogging the face off the fattest woman you have ever seen. She was even holding a plate of chips and curry sauce in one hand and her handbag in the other. Lisa's mates were teasing her, saying to just go home with me and get a good shagging.

I was a little embarrassed to say the least so I just stood there smiling. Lisa asked where I lived, I said just around the corner and I asked if she fancied a drink at mine. She took her time replying but one of her friends just decided for her and said she would.

She came back to mine and we opened some wine and we sat on the sofa just chilling and chatting. I remember having a chill out album on in the background and we smoked some weed. Lisa had never smoked weed before and she was so funny. After her coughing fit she just had the giggles. We stayed like that all night, I didn't even make a move on her, and I didn't want to, I didn't want to ruin it.

We spent the next day together then she stayed at mine again and we ended up in bed together. I thought she would be more experienced in that department, more assertive but she just let me carry on. She was very affectionate. Lisa is a very beautiful woman and it was such a good feeling to wake up next to her the next morning. I even took a sick day on the Monday and we just stayed in bed.

We started seeing each other properly. We would see each other maybe once in the week and then more over the weekend. We both loved movies and we would happily snuggle up and watch a movie together. Not horror's though, she wasn't keen on those, which given what was happening in her life makes perfect sense. If you ever date someone and they don't like horror movies I'd find out first if there is anything strange going on in their lives, seriously, you never know do you?

Lisa always came to mine. I never went to her house for close to a year. I didn't mind as it was easier for me, I worked in Haverfordwest so I didn't have to rush off as much in the morning. Lisa worked shifts, so some days she didn't have to be there till noon or later in the afternoon.

Time passed on and it was good, really good. I liked to cook back then and she was happy to eat and we would pop down the pub and have a few pints or just have some wine at home. One weekend I had been invited to a party down her neck of the woods so I invited her and she was happy to come. She laughed and asked would people think that I had brought my mother along? I didn't care about the age gap, besides she was only in her mid-thirties and she looked great. My mate commented that I had bagged a M.I.L.F., Lisa was fine about it though. I asked if perhaps we could stay at hers after the party. She went white as a sheet and looked away. She couldn't look me in the eye. I was concerned, you know? You automatically begin to think the worst sometimes. Years before I had really fallen for this girl I had met in work. We had gotten on so well and we ended up together. There were a few people who were a bit funny about us seeing each other but I didn't care as I was so into this girl. It all makes sense now; I wish they had just told me. This girl and I were out all the time, she said she loved me and we were even going to move in together. She went away for Christmas to see her family and on Boxing Day told me it was over between us as her boyfriend was back! I was shocked. She'd had a boyfriend the whole time, he'd been travelling Europe for a year. I wasn't sure who I was sorrier for, him or me. The crazy fucker even asked if we were still going to get a place together and could he move in with us. I was gutted.

 I took a deep breath and I asked Lisa why? I was beginning to dread that maybe she was married or was with someone. A million things whizzed through my mind, maybe she was ashamed of where she lived or maybe her son didn't know about me. She started crying and I just held her so tight and she felt so weak and fragile.

I calmed her down and we sat on the sofa, she told me it was complicated and that I wouldn't understand. I asked her to tell me, whatever she had to say, I would listen, and I would try to understand. You think of the most berserk things imaginable. She looked me in the eye and she told me she loved me and never wanted to lose me.

I told her she wouldn't and I would be here for her, forever. Then she told me. She told me her house was haunted.

I almost laughed. I'm not laughing now, obviously, but I remember my reaction was to just laugh and tell her not to be silly. I shut up though and she told me it had been really bad and how several times she'd tried to get a new home. She told me that terrible things had happened there. She wouldn't go into detail and she said nothing had happened in the last few years. She was scared that if I went there it would all start again. I was intrigued and a little excited, I liked the paranormal, I wasn't massively into it but I liked hearing about it and watching T.V programmes and films about it. It started to make sense as to why she always stayed at mine and how she never liked horror movies.

 I reassured her and told her that I wouldn't force the subject. I said that I didn't have to stay but I would look after her, I loved her and I wouldn't let anything happen to her. She didn't say anything, she just hugged me and I hugged her back. I whispered into her ear that everything would be ok, everything would be fine.

God, I was wrong, I was so terribly wrong.

Uninvited

As I sat by Daniel by the river I realised just how damaged he was. Here was a man who had witnessed something incomprehensible while trying to suppress the feeling for a woman whose circumstance have made it impossible for them to ever be happy together. Lisa was a woman who still resided in his heart. Lisa has designated herself as the perpetrator of the wrong doing but really what choice did she have in the matter? Some may argue that she connived and concealed the truth from Daniel, but at the time of their meeting the haunting had subsided greatly. One cannot label hope as a crime, the hope that the supernatural intrusion was over, never to return.

I believe Lisa did not perform some masquerade to entice Daniel into her life, pretending she was something she wasn't. She and Dan settled into a warm and loving routine and she simply, as many people do, had a dark and terrible secret. Who would you tell if this happened to you? Would you be confident that you could broach the subject during the early stages of a blossoming relationship? Would you take the risk of having questionable mental health? How would you choose the words to describe what had happened or would you simply blurt out, I have been a sexually assaulted by a ghost?

It is an undesirable position to be in and hopefully many of you reading this will never have to concern yourself with this dilemma. The only time I wish for this subject to ever be a part of your life is while indulging in this account and while maybe posing the question to your friends and family. I think we all need to try and empathise with Lisa and those close to her who have been affected so we can understand the emotional complexity of the situation. As stated we are all investigators of her account and nothing more. For that I am thankful and you are blessed.

This next section presented is the fusion from Daniels account and Lisa's testimonial. This will give a much more comprehensive insight into the events that eventually dissolved the relationship between the two. The events to be described leave me asking how Daniel still has a functioning mind. He claims to have been part of something which was loathsome and depressing yet he does not detest Lisa, he simply cannot fully assimilate the events into a fashion that makes sense to him. It is beyond my comprehension that he is even able to speak about the abhorrence which follows.

Lisa: Daniel asked if he could stay at mine. There was a party in Pembroke and it was only a few miles from my house. I was dumbfounded. He had never asked and I never offered. I felt so safe and relaxed at his little flat in

Haverfordwest. It wasn't a massive place and probably too small for two people to live there all the time together plus there would be nowhere for Tyler to stay if he ever needed to come home. I was so happy with Daniel there. I felt for the first time in my life truly different. I felt reborn. I didn't mind being at my house so much as not only was it quiet there now but I had something to look forward to in going to see Daniel.

I relaxed to the extent that Tyler got his own place, not too far, but he had quite a well-paid job and besides he was old enough to do what he wanted. He had a girl staying with him most of the time so I didn't want to cramp his style. I did miss him and glad he's back now.

One night I had a terrible nightmare that something was in the bedroom. It was pitch black, something was pulling off the duvet and I couldn't scream or move. It was like I was blind and paralysed. I thought it was happening again. I woke up, drenched in sweat and panting, but it was morning. The sun was shining behind the curtains. I cried so much, I think more with relief than anything.

I never heard any creaks or bangs in the night. No bad smells or temperature changes. There was nothing at all to cause me concern. It was good and I allowed myself to relax. I allowed myself to be happy. I imagine some people would question how I can go out with a man again or live in that house but what else is there to do? Hide away, alone till I die? Daniel was the best thing that had ever happened to me since Tyler was born and was different from Ian and Leon. He was there, he was available. Always just a bus away or a text. He had been very open about his life. There was no family living away up North or parents that hated me. It was just us and it was wonderful while it lasted. I just wish, I just wish I had put my foot down and never let him come to my house.

Daniel: We went to this party and it was O.K, nothing special but Lisa and I had a good time and Kev turned up around eleven, drunk, and was dancing and falling around the place. Lisa looked great that night, she had bought a new top and jeans and she looked lovely. I just wanted to get her home to bed but she was in no rush to get home. I don't think she drank all night; she had a bottle of beer and just held it. She got more and more anxious as the night went on. When it got dark I could see in her face that she was concerned. I remember taking her to one side, away from the other people at the party and telling her to just relax and I would look after her, then we had a long intimate and loving kiss. You know, the one's you never want to end. The sort of Kiss that makes you forget everything in the world and you feel attached, like one with that person. She held me so tight. I loved her so much.

Lisa: At the Party Daniel sensed that I was nervous and he was great, he really knew my moods and how to re-act. He told me everything would be O.K. but I didn't want to leave. I never wanted the party to end, not that it was any good, I just didn't want to go home. There were a lot of people there and the ones we spoke to were really nice. I smoked some weed in the garden with Daniel and a couple he knew and after that I relaxed a bit. Can I just say that I am not a habitual marijuana smoker; I smoked it just three times since I met Daniel. Drink and cigarettes have always been enough for me. I like it and I don't think it does much harm in my opinion but I don't want people thinking I am some type of pot head or druggy. I don't like not being in control and certainly wouldn't want to try anything harder than weed. I would hate for people to think well all of this is shit because she is on drugs all the time.

Daniel: We must have left around 2 a.m. It was late, I was a little drunk but not paralytic. Kev was being sick in the garden when we left and about half the party had gone home. Lisa said we were about twenty minutes away from her house and wanted to know if we should walk or get a taxi. I felt fine to walk and she said it was a nice night so we walked. She seemed relieved and I guessed it was because she was still uncomfortable with the idea of me being at her house. We were walking past this wooded area on the way to hers and Lisa grabbed me by hand and led me into the trees. You could still see the road and the street lights but we were hidden from sight and she just started kissing me. She knelt down and unzipped by trousers and started to suck me off. I was so surprised not that I was complaining, it was awesome. I came and she stood up and just hugged me. I asked her what that was all about and she said when we got home could we just sleep? I said of course we can and I laughed and said she didn't have to give me a gobble just so I would go straight to bed. Looking back, it all makes so much sense. She did it as she was scared that once we got to hers I would try it on with her, she didn't know how the things that were in there would react.

We got to her house and it was an ordinary council house that you see in Pembrokeshire at the end of a road. The house was white and bathed in the orange of the street light, behind the house there looked to be fields or woodland. It seemed nice enough and nothing at all to be worried about. It wasn't some big old creepy mansion with a creaking gate and forked lightening going off over it. It was just a plain house.

Lisa seemed hesitant to open the door and when she tried she ended up dropping the keys. Her hands were shaking and I just looked at her and said it was O.K and to just relax. She opened the door and the hallway was dark and she quickly turned on the light. The house was nice, it was clean and pleasant and there was no feeling of foreboding. The way she was I expected something in a white sheet to dart out at us. That would have been a lot easier to deal with to be honest.

Lisa: We got home and the house was quiet. I asked Daniel if he wanted anything and I made us a coffee. I was so jittery. I felt like I was trespassing or doing something wrong. I spoke to Daniel in whispers almost as if I didn't want us to be heard. I just hoped Daniel wouldn't do anything stupid like taunt the house or go on about the ghost. Daniel was sat on the settee and I put on the T.V, there was a late night movie on and I went and sat in this armchair. Daniel asked if wanted to snuggle with him on the settee but at first I didn't want him to touch me, I didn't want him to be close as I didn't want to make anything get jealous or angry. Then Daniel asked if he could use the loo and I nearly said to go in the garden. I had to be strong and I had to push the negativity away and believe it was all over. I couldn't let this ruin my life with Daniel but as you can understand I was terrified, not only that it would come back and assault me again, but that I would lose Daniel as well. I walked him to the bottom of the stairs, put on the landing light and told him it was straight up the stairs. My heart was pounding in my chest.

Daniel: I went upstairs and it felt perfectly fine up there. On the landing I could see into what I then presumed was Lisa's bedroom and it seemed nice enough. It looked like she had spent the day hoovering and polishing. I am the sort of person that expects no fuss. I'm not there to see how you live, just there to see you. I went to the toilet and I had a gigantic piss. The sort that just never wants to end, you know, like a racehorse?

I flushed the chain and washed my hands and came back onto the landing, then I saw a shadow move in Lisa's bedroom. Just a streak of darkness pass between the light of the landing and the light painted walls in there. I thought she was in there; maybe putting on her pyjama's or something so I popped my head in and there was no one, nothing at all moving in there. I heard Lisa call up the stairs asking if I was O.K and I shouted down that I was fine. I did feel a bit excited and I got a few goose bumps but then I started to think that the power of suggestion is a powerful thing. I knew that the house was allegedly haunted and I had been drinking and smoked some green and if you added Lisa's nervousness then suddenly you are going to start seeing and imagining things. If you went to someone's house and they said it was haunted then you would expect to see something or hear something. You hear a creak and it's a ghost, you see a shadow and it's a ghost but if you went to the same house and were not told then would you jump to such drastic conclusions? You would just think that the creak was the house settling and the shadow was caused by a light outsight or something rational. That's what I thought that night and I didn't mention it to Lisa, why would I? She was jittery enough. You have to realize as well that at this stage I had been told it was just a haunting, I was not told about the repulsive assaults. If I had known then I would have told her, but then again if I had known would I have stayed with her at all? Would any of this have happened? I guess we will never know but one thing for sure was that it wouldn't take long for me to believe, it wouldn't take long for it to ruin me.

Lisa: It was such a relief the next morning when we woke up on the settee all wrapped up in each other's arms. I felt fine and Daniel just had these red blood shot eyes and asked had he been eating carpet all night as his mouth was as dry as a fuck without foreplay. He was so funny back then; it makes me sad to think of how he is now.

Daniel: Things were fine for a time. I stayed over a few times but I noticed how Lisa always tried to get us to sleep on the settee but it was uncomfortable. I reasoned with her just to go to bed, that I was there and we would be fine and if she wanted the light on then that would be fine too.

I even met Tyler. He's a nice guy but a bit of a waster. He just needs to focus and try and do something with his life but that's his business. Lisa has mothered him too much and now he knows he doesn't have to commit to anything as he always has her to fall back on, especially when it comes to money. Two weeks after I met him he bluntly asked if I could lend him a hundred quid. I said no and he was a bit sulky with me for a bit.

It was nice to have a change from my flat. Lisa's house had a garden and it was summer so I made salads and dinners that we could eat out in the sun. It was lush. I even noticed that Lisa started to relax more about the house. She didn't seem as anxious all the time.

I didn't see any more shadows or sense anything but I think it started not long after I had an awful nightmare that still haunts me. We went to bed. Lisa and I had started to have sex at hers. Nothing rampant, we kept that for my place but gentle, loving sex. We were always covered up in the duvet and she hardly made any noise at all, not like when she was at mine. I hardly ever saw her naked at her house, as soon as she was out of the shower she put her clothes on under her towel like you do when you are at the beach.

That night we had sex; she kept her top on and just pulled her knickers to one side so I could penetrate her. It was still amazing; to be inside her and be close and just hold her tight. I liked it. After sex I slept and I had this awful dream, not a dream a nightmare. I dreamt I woke up and I could see the bedroom in the gloom, I was at Lisa's not mine or anyone else's and I could feel the warmth of someone next to me and a soft breathing, I looked and I could see the back of Lisa's head on her pillow as she slept.

Suddenly it wet freezing cold. My face was freezing and I inhaled deep cold breaths like it was a frosty winter's day. Then I felt this cold, hard hand cover my nose and mouth and I couldn't breathe. The cold hand felt like it was crushing my face, trying to squeeze it off. I couldn't move, couldn't scream and It felt as if my lungs were filling with painful and jagged frost and were about to explode. I thought I was dying and the pain was insane.

I woke up screaming and gasping for breath. Lisa jumped up and put on the light and just stared at me and screamed *are you O.K? What's happening?* I was coughing and shaking. Once I got my composure back I told her about the dream. She looked as white as a sheet especially when I explained about the coldness and the pain and the freezing air in my lungs. She said it was just a bad dream, she grabbed my face and just buried me in her chest and held me for ages. It was a terrible dream, when I woke it was almost as if I could feel the pain and cold still on my face. I felt like I had stopped breathing. I thought I was going to die. It was the worst nightmare ever.

Lisa: I couldn't believe what he was telling me. I had never told him about the cold and freezing feelings. I dreaded this was real and I prayed it was only a dream ...but one thing scared me so much... I grabbed his head and just hugged him to stop him getting up and going to the bathroom or anything, to stop him seeing anything... he had a big red handprint across his face, across his nose and mouth, exactly as he had described in his dream. I could only hope that he had somehow done it to himself but I think we know who was behind it. I'm not sure to this day if Daniel knows about the handprint. I don't think he could cope knowing that it tried to suffocate him in his sleep. I think he would be in a worse state than he is already if he knew that it actually tried to kill him.

Daniel: No, I didn't think it was anything more than a dream. Why would I? You're not telling me that was part of it as well are you? Oh my god, did it try to fucking kill me? This is awful, this is insane. Why would it do that? Was it jealous? FUCK! I'm glad I'm out of there. Is Lisa safe? This is so much to take in. There is no way it would try and kill me; it was just a dream! It was just a fucking dream, I know that crazy berserk shit was happening, I saw some weird things but that was just a dream and it would be ludicrous for us all to jump to these crazy conclusions that the was anything else to it. I think we need to focus on what we saw, what we know to be real. This is insane enough as it is, without thinking it was trying to kill people. That it was trying to kill me. I'm moving on from that O.K! I would appreciate it if you don't mention it again to me.

One night we were at mine, it was a couple of months after the dream. Lisa had been very anxious, she tried to persuade me not to come over as often but I liked it at hers, as I said, I liked the garden plus I had friends in Pembroke and we would visit them, so it was nice just to stay at hers. I will admit I never saw any more shadows or felt anything while I was there that particular time and didn't have any more strange dreams. Well nothing happened at hers for a bit anyway.

We were at my place and we had a good night, watched some movies and we had sex. I liked to snuggle up with Lisa after sex but eventually I get hot and I would turn on my side and face the wall so my back is to her.

Lisa: That night we made love and we went to sleep. I remember waking up in the night, it was pitch black, I felt something and I was thinking, oh my god I'm going to cum, I was really close to orgasm and it was such an intense feeling. Daniel was quite frisky and sometimes I would wake up and he would be feeling me up or rubbing his erection against my behind and sometimes we would make love or if I was tired then I would tell him to behave and go to sleep. This was really, really good and I could feel my whole body trembling. The nerves around my clit felt like a current was running through them. First there was a tingling that intensified, then there was a short sharp intense increase and then I climaxed. It was such a very intense pulsing which felt like my clit was trying to turn itself inside out and instead of lasting only a few seconds it lasted for an age and then a throb, throb, throb... then I had the biggest gush I had ever had. I had no idea what was happening. I actually screamed my head off in pleasure.

Dan: Lisa woke me, she was screaming and laughing and I dived out of bed. I didn't know where I was or what was happening. I turned on the light and Lisa was lying there with her arms across her face. She was sweating and breathing heavy and the duvet was pulled down and her breasts were exposed.

I asked her was she *O.K?* To which she panted, *I'm amazing* and said *thank you* and asked *what new trick had I learned?*

I was so confused and I just looked at her. I hadn't touched her. I thought she had been strumming one off in her sleep. I asked had she been masturbating. She just laughed and said no and asked if I had cum too? I told her I hadn't even touched her and she looked bemused. She looked at me and quickly put her hand down under the duvet and then between her legs and she screamed. Not in joy this time but in absolute terror.

Lisa: Dan said he hadn't touched me, said he had been asleep. I thought that maybe he had touched me or had sex with me in my sleep or maybe I had touched myself and hadn't realized. My knees were trembling, this had been the best orgasm of my life to this point and Dan wasn't taking the credit. I started to think, no way, not here, it couldn't be, I was at Daniels Flat. I started to fear the worse. I put my hands on myself, on my vagina and I screamed. I felt so ashamed and mortified. It was numb and ice-cold.

Daniel: Lisa kept screaming and screaming and I asked her what was wrong, I asked her to be quiet, it was 3 a.m. and I didn't want her to wake the people next door. She screamed and screamed. I panicked and I pulled off the duvet and what I saw, what was there was so startling, so confusing.

Lisa: Daniel Just ripped off the duvet and I lay there naked with my hands on my vagina and the entire colour from his face just drained. I never saw him so shocked until that point. He just stood there, dressed in only his boxer shorts, just staring. I looked down and I just wailed. All over my legs, all up my thighs and all around my genitals were great big red handprints. They were Large, brutish marks, fading, but evident. I ran into the bathroom and sat there against the door while Daniel stood on the landing and asked a million times if I was O.K? I sat there sobbing, not replying, the marks and the numbness eventually disappearing. I couldn't believe it.

Whatever it was, what ever had been doing this...It was back and it had followed me.

Triumvirate

Lisa: You have no idea how much of a shock it was? What it did at Daniels flat. I can't explain it but I somehow knew that it would get me where ever I was. I knew that it wasn't just my house. I cannot explain to you further than that on why I felt that way. I just knew it was always with me. I don't know why it chose to do it to me there and then and not in the toilets where I work or the short cut through some woods that I would take home sometimes in the summer. I think it was sending me a message. To remind me that it wasn't gone and that it could get me anywhere at any time. It was reminding me that I still belonged to it.

I can't explain how it knew where to go. I thought that maybe it just kept tabs on me or maybe was always with me, just waiting to gain enough energy to touch me. Maybe it has been with me forever or maybe there was a time in my life when I was so vulnerable that it just attached itself to me. What you have to think about is that something like this might not be individual, in that there is more than one, maybe these things can attach themselves to any person at any one time. Someone reading or hearing this might think *I'm glad it didn't happen to me*, but what's not to say that it might one day happen to them? One day life is normal. You work, you have family and you are happy and then from nowhere and without warning you are being abused sexually by something we can't understand yet.

Poor Daniel was so confused by everything, and he just stood on the landing while I sat on his bathroom floor sobbing. I felt so dirty, so ashamed. I let my guard down. I thought I was safe. I thought I would be O.K at Daniels and I came and it was the biggest and most intense orgasm I had ever had. I feel so very ashamed, I felt so angry with myself but you have to understand that I thought it was Daniel, the man I had been with for eighteen months at the time. The man I loved.

Daniel: When that happened I had no idea what was going on. I didn't think it was anything to do with the haunting. I just thought it was something Lisa had done to herself. No one else had been in the house, I checked that, and I certainly hadn't done that to her. I did doubt myself that maybe I had touched her in my sleep, you know like sleep walking but with sex? Lisa must have locked herself in my bathroom for hours, just sobbing away.

I started to think that maybe something had happened in her life, something from her past. Maybe she had been abused or been the victim of incest or perhaps raped. Whatever it was I thought I would not turn my back on her. I wanted to support her. Whatever it was, I didn't care, I love her, I mean loved her. Everyone has a past right? Everyone has secrets and she and I had been together so long that we could work through it; I arrogantly believed I could help her.

At this time I didn't know about the sexual assaults by *spirits* or *ghosts* or whatever they were. I just thought she had some type of episode, some sort of breakdown.

Lisa: I watched the marks on my legs disappear and the numbness in my fanny went. In that moment the last thing you think of is taking a picture. If you saw a picture of handprints on my body would you have believed a ghost had touched me? I didn't think so. I was in shock and I was still trembling from the orgasm. I felt like I had cheated on Dan. I felt like I was a whore. How could I tell him it was a ghost? How could I tell him that something was following me around and sexually assaulting me? How could I tell him that a ghost had fucked me and I had just enjoyed it? I did the only thing I could think of to protect our relationship. I lied.

Daniel: Lisa eventually came out of the bathroom. She was covered in towels. She wouldn't let me look at her body; she just gave me a big hug. Her whole body was trembling and I squeezed her so hard and I whispered to her that everything was O.K.

She led me back to the bedroom and we sat on the bed. She looked at me and said that when she was a teenager she would have these sleep panic attacks and sometimes she would hurt herself but sometimes she would masturbate too, really frantically and wake up thinking someone had just had sex with her. She said she hadn't had one in over twenty years and she was sorry for the way she reacted as it had been a shock as it had been so long since it had last happened. She said she would claw and mark herself while doing so and when she was younger her Mum had to take her to a doctor and for a while she had to take sedatives before bed. She said she didn't know why it had happened again and thought maybe it was due to smoking the weed or maybe hormonal changes in her body. She said she would go to the Doctor and have a chat.

I held her and said that everything would be O.K. I was relived to be honest as I wasn't sure if it was me that had done it and I didn't want people to think I was some kind of sleep rapist or bedtime molester.

Lisa: We went back to bed and I tried to hide my fear and confusion. I had no idea how it had done this. I couldn't afford to tell Daniel. I couldn't lose him.

Daniel: I don't think anything happened for a few weeks. Lisa had said she had gone to the Doctors and hoped it wouldn't happen again but she said there were no guarantees, but at least I was aware of it. At least it wouldn't be such a shock again.

Lisa: About a month later we were at mine and we went to bed. We didn't make love or anything that night. I think we had, had a bottle or two of red and we staggered up to bed and just collapsed in a heap. I woke up in the night and it was happening again, I couldn't move, I felt literally frozen and I could feel myself so close to climax and then I came, same as before, powerful and intense. Once I came it just suddenly vanished and I was free to move. I didn't scream and I didn't cry, I didn't do anything, I just lay there, my heart racing as Daniel lay next to me snoring. I wanted to shout. I wanted to dash up and put the light on but I lay there and I said nothing. Is it wrong? I could have woke Daniel up and told him I had, had another episode or I could just lie there and he wouldn't know any different.

I have to admit that lying there in the darkness next to Daniel that I felt like I was having an affair and I felt so sorry for Daniel. He was oblivious to it. I was worried that he would wake me up and maybe feel me down there and feel the icy coldness of where this thing had been.

It was obviously different from the shitty man and I was so grateful for that but it was still wrong. I still had no choice in the matter. It was still rape.

Dan: I never knew until later how frequently it had been going on. I didn't know that it was a regular occurrence until I witnessed it myself. I was oblivious but I did get the sense, especially at Lisa's that I was not a welcome presence in her house.

There was an incident when I was locked in the bathroom. I couldn't get out, it was like someone was holding the door from the other side and the handle to the door was freezing cold and then the door suddenly opened. It was such a stupid situation to be in as Lisa and I were hiding things like this from each other. Neither of us was mentioning the alleged antics for fear of upsetting the other.

One night I woke up and the bedroom was pitch black, there wasn't even the street light from behind the curtains. I was so disorientated; I was so confused that I actually for a second thought I had gone blind. You know when you wake up and you have no idea what is going on? I used to wake up in the night when I was younger and I had slept on my arm and I couldn't feel it, it had gone numb, and I would be convinced that it would be chopped off as I had lost all circulation. When you wake up you can just think stupid stuff like that. I wake up and its pitch black. I hear this weird high pitch noise in the room, like an electrical device, and then from the side cabinet my mobile phone gently starts glowing. Not like I'm getting a call or a message but just like something is interfering with it. It happened a few times there. I know it doesn't sound like the most terrifying thing but it did freak me out.

I remember throwing a pillow across the room one night. I woke up and again it was pitch black, maybe the street light outside had a fault, but my phone was glowing slightly by the side of the bed. I used to think that was like a sign that something was in the room. I looked around the room and as the phone glowed I thought I saw a figure of a man move from the doorway and to the foot of the bed. I panicked and threw the closest thing to hand; a pillow. Like a pillow would protect us? I scrambled and put on the light and Lisa was asleep next to me and I just stared wide eyed into the room. There was no one there. I turned the light off and guess what? The street light is shining in from behind the curtain. I started to believe that the house was definitely haunted but I still hadn't linked it to Lisa's sexual episode.

I am not ashamed to admit that when I was younger, probably up to my mid teenage years that I was absolutely afraid of the dark. I hated it. I always used to have my light on and my sisters would always mock me. I just hated it; it wasn't so much the dark itself but what could lurk in the dark. There could be anything in it, and I felt vulnerable, at a disadvantage. As I grew older it phased out but I would always try and have a clock radio or my phone by the side of the bed, you know a comfort thing?

There was an evening where Lisa and I had been out with friends and I had been drinking. Not a huge amount but enough that as soon as we got back to hers that I had to have a pint of water before bed. In the night I needed a pee and I clambered out of bed. It was light in the room because of the streetlight and I headed onto the landing and into the bathroom. I put on the light and started to have a slash. Then the light went out. Now there was always some ambient light from outside the bathroom window but it was dark, really dark. You lose night vision after having the light on but this was dark. I couldn't see anything and I will be honest that I started to panic; I felt disorientated and closed in. I felt something was in there with me. I could imagine awful hands reaching out for me. I could almost hear something breathing in there. I nearly screamed and then the light just flickered back on. Maybe there had been a power cut or maybe being half drunk and in the dark that I had some type of anxiety attack.

I seem to say the words that *I felt,* all the time but it's the best way to describe what was happening. I don't have any video footage or photo's, only the way it made me feel and I did *feel* that it was making itself known to me. Maybe it was toying with me; maybe it was trying to push me out or maybe it wanted me to know it was there watching Lisa and I. It was there stood in the dark just watching us as we slept. It was there silent and patient conserving its energy so it could really, really makes itself known and what I witnessed that night was unbelievable. It was deplorable and depressing and no one will ever understand what happened to me that night. It affected me for the rest of my life.

Lisa: I guessed it had been focused on Daniel as well as me. One night we were in Bed, we had been asleep maybe a few hours and I woke up and it was happening again, the ghost sex. There was the same icy cold feeling and the build-up of an orgasm. There was never any weight or roughness like in the early days and another thing I had noticed was that it was happening regardless of what I was wearing. It was as if things in our world were not a problem or barrier. So if I had my underwear on or was fully clothed if would still do its thing to me. I was there paralysed and cumming and I didn't want to wake Dan and as I came I gave a little moan and my whole body trembled as I was released from its grip. I lay there breathing quite heavily and the next thing I heard was Daniel saying, *I don't mind doing that for you.* He had been awake the whole time and thought I was just masturbating. I lied to him and said that if I had known he was awake that he could have done it for me and then he started to kiss me and climbed on top of me and we had sex. He even said I was *freezing down there* and that he could *warm it up* with his *tongue* but I just told him to shag me. I had to try and enjoy him but it was not the same, it was not the same experience as before besides the last thing I wanted was sex. I faked an orgasm and he came and he lay beside me and was soon asleep. I am not the sort of person to have multiple partners, to have threesome or gang bangs or whatever they are called but that was what it felt like that night. I started to feel like an object to be used for sex at a whim. It wasn't Daniels fault, I loved him, but I became less and less interested in sex with him the more the supernatural entity had sex with me.

I couldn't stop the intruder, I couldn't so I took it out on Daniel and it was a terrible thing to do to him. The only person I could control sex with was Dan. He had always been so loving and attentive but I couldn't stand the thought of sex with two partners. Sex should be something special shared between two people and not shared by a third invader. How would you feel if your partner had sex with someone immediately after they had sex with you? Would it turn you on? Would it make you feel inadequate? Would you feel that you were not enough or that there was no emotional connection? I believe that sex is a personal and emotional experience that should be shared by two people that have that connection. If you want to go out and have lots of sex with different people then be single and do it, don't destroy the trust of someone who thinks the world of you and that loves you unconditionally. I felt like I was cheating on Daniel and to make it worse I was punishing him for the violation that the spirit was undertaking. I was stopping that physicality between us. It was such a messed up situation.

Dan was getting more and more frustrated and concerned, not just in terms of the lack of closeness between us but because I think the ghost was putting more attention on him, making him paranoid and uncomfortable. Daniel actually started to come around to mine much less and even said that it wasn't because we weren't having sex as much but because he didn't feel comfortable staying there like he used too. The house did seem to have a darker presence. You know when there has been an argument and there is that tension in the house; that silence? Well that was what it was like. There was an atmosphere there.

I was losing Daniel and we would have stupid rows over such little things. One night we had a few drinks and we had a row over nothing and Daniel stormed off and got a taxi home. I got it into my head he was flirting with some girl and I went home and I was so hurt and angry with him. I went to bed and woke up and the entity was at me again and I feel so awful for this, I feel such a terrible human being but I was glad and I felt like I was teaching Daniel a lesson for the way he treated me that night. I think...I enjoyed it and after I came I cried and cried. I felt terrible. I remember one woman I worked with wasn't getting on with her husband and they had a huge row and she went out that night and shagged some stranger. She said she did it to hurt her husband but she regretted it and he ended up finding out and that was the end of the marriage. She said she did it as she felt as if she didn't exist anymore and she needed to feel desirable, to feel wanted. I felt the same way; I felt I was having an affair. I was having an affair with something that wasn't even human. I am a despicable person. Every day the guilt runs deep and how that man had to suffer, a good man that would never have hurt me or cheated on me. The moment I let myself enjoy the spirit sex was the moment I ruined what Daniel and I had. It is awful what I put Dan through. I never told him about that night but I didn't have to. He had to witness much worse, Dan had to watch as it fucked me and he has never been the same since. We have never been the same since.

Daniel: The night it happened, it was horrendous. I can't explain how such things happen and it has made me question everything. Before I was just a man with an ordinary life, just taking everything for granted and now I can't sleep at night worrying that thing will get me and knowing what it is doing to Lisa. When we are younger we are taught about God and Jesus. I wasn't from a particularly religious back ground but we learned enough in junior school for me to believe that there was a God.

I actually enjoyed religious studies. The stories were great when you are a kid. I believed in Jesus and all the miraculous things he did. Now I don't know if I believe at all. If there was a God or a Christ then how could they allow such evil to stalk people of this earth? How are they allowed to do to people as they will? What happened to Lisa and to me, we didn't deserve. It is a demon, a monster from Hell and God is just letting it happen. I used think for there to be a hell then there has to be a heaven, but what if there is just a hell? There is just a hell from which these creatures pass into our world and torture us and treat us like inconsequential life forms.

I have had a long time to think about this and I don't think it is a spirit or a ghost as Lisa call's it. I have done research and there are encounters with demons that have sexual intercourse with people. They are called Incubus and Succubus among other things. This is what I believe it to be and Lisa has let herself enjoy the pleasures of these things and she is letting them take her soul. When I die, I just want to die and for there to be nothing. I am comfortable with that. I don't want a heaven or to be re-incarnated, I just want there to be nothing, so I am done with these things. I never want to experience anything like this again but every waking moment I think will *it try and get me today?* That is the only way that I will be ever free from its grasp. If I was not so cowardly then I would have taken my own life. I swear to you know that I have these thoughts on a daily basis. I hate it, I hate it! Why did I ever have to meet her!

Lisa: The night it happened, I can't imagine how Daniel must have felt. I cry sometimes, even after all this time, to think of him having to see me like that.

Daniel: Imagine that well of anguish you get in your stomach when something goes wrong in your life or that hollow, cold feeling in your chest when you know that the person you love no longer loves you and it's over. I have that feeling every day. It's like I am constantly heart broken.

Lisa: We went to bed as normal. I don't think Daniel was planning to stay that night but I asked him to and we were at that stage that I went to bed before him and he sat downstairs on his own watching T.V. I had killed the intimacy between us, Daniel had not done anything wrong, but it was too much to have both. There was a blur to who was who and I couldn't distinguish anymore. Daniel was still good to me but there was no physicality any more. We hadn't had sex in months. The crazy thing is, is that Daniel is such a good man that I would never have accused him or suspected him to cheat on me. I was starving him of an important part of our relationship but I knew he wouldn't hunger for it in the arms of another woman. He could have back then; he was handsome and charming still, not grey and broken as he is now. He was so loyal and loving. God, that poor man has been through so much.

Daniel: I was watching T.V downstairs, Lisa had gone to bed. I wasn't watching anything in particular. I was missing my friends and the freedom I used to have but I still loved Lisa and I had no idea to why she was so turned off to me. I had always tried to be a loving and attentive partner. I hoped it was just some phase and it would pass and we would be back to how it was. It was a Friday night, past twelve and I thought I had better get up to bed. I turned off the T.V and headed on up in the stairs. I knew the house well enough to not have the lights on and there was always a little light from the street through the front of the house. When I got to the top of the landing it got really dark again, like the dark was engulfing me, covering me. I felt panicky, and this freezing coldness just swept over me. I stood there, literally frozen with all my hair standing on end. I felt something sweep across my neck and I gave out a screech and I just found the energy to dash into Lisa's bedroom. I jumped into bed and lay there with the Duvet over my head. I tried to snuggle as close to her as possible, but since we had stopped having sex, she had this habit of sleeping with her elbows facing out. Almost like a barrier to stop me getting close to her.

I lay there expecting the door to open or the duvet to be pulled off but there was nothing. There was just my panicked breathing. Somehow I managed to drop off and wish I had never woke up. I don't even know how to explain this. You are just going to think I am mad. I feel like a lunatic just thinking about what I am about to tell you.

When I woke it was still dark and I heard this weird moaning noise. I sat up quickly and turned on the light. I looked over and Lisa was lying there on her back with her eyes open but not moving. The duvet was off her and she was just lying there in her pyjamas. She didn't look at me or anything but was making this weird moaning sound. I thought that maybe she was having one of those weird night terror things she had suffered from before.

Then, I swear to you, her pyjama top started to rise up on its own. I was so confused to how she could do this. I asked her if she was *O.K.* But she never answered; she just had these dead, lifeless eyes. I tried to touch her and then I was covered in that awful cold feeling again. This time it was intense and I felt an icy sharp pain on either side of my face and down into my neck. I could not move at all, it was if I was paralysed. It was so painful. I felt like my head was in a vice. I watched as Lisa's pyjama bottoms were slowly pulled off. It was like someone was at the foot of the bed and was pulling them off.

Something invisible was undressing her. Her legs slowly spread and Lisa made a louder moan. She still had her underwear on but I could see red marks appearing on her thighs. I just wanted to grab her and drag her out of there. I couldn't, I couldn't help her, I let it touch her, and I let it molest her.

It was as if it wanted me to watch her being sexually assaulted. It was as if it was displaying its power. It knew I could do nothing. How would you like to see someone you loved raped before your very eyes and there is nothing you can do to stop it? I was in that position for ages. I couldn't scream but only make weird moaning, gurgling sounds. I was dribbling all down my neck and onto my chest. This is awful, this is so sickening. I saw... I saw a bulge in Lisa's belly, like something was inside her, pushing out from within. It was under her skin, almost throbbing and then my eyes welled up with tears and then everything was blurred. There was something inside of her and every time it protruded, Lisa would moan, like she was having sex.

This lasted for ages and I just shut my eyes. I gave up. The pain in my face and neck and the image of Lisa being assaulted like that was too much. Then I felt my head being pushed closer to Lisa's, by some unseen force, and then she screamed and I was suddenly released and lay face down on the pillow sobbing. The icy cold feeling disappeared and I couldn't comprehend what had happened. It wasn't a dream. I had just watched the woman I loved get raped.

Lisa: I only ever had Daniels account of what it was doing to me. I woke up and I was cumming again, this time it was different, it was incredibly powerful like every nerve ending in my body was on fire and I screamed. I sat up, scared that Dan would have heard me .The light was on and Daniel was lying next to me. He was crying like a baby. I sat up and I grabbed him and he flung my arm away from him. He looked at me; his face was wet and his eyes red. He got out of bed and grabbed his clothes and stormed out of the bedroom. I chased after him and caught up with him at the bottom of the stairs. He was frantically putting on his clothes. He opened the front door and I begged him to tell me what had happened. I knew what had happened but I didn't know what he had seen. He turned and quietly said Lisa, *you were just raped by a ghost* and he left the house. He left me alone and I sat on the bottom steps of the stairs and wailed and wailed.

Daniel: I had to leave, I just had to. Can you even begin to imagine the thoughts whizzing around my mind at this time? I was confused beyond belief. Was I insane? Had I been spiked? Maybe it was a nightmare? I couldn't figure out and I didn't want to know to be honest. Lisa had lied to me, she had withheld what had been happening to her and had said it was a sleep condition. She had lied for nearly two years about this and all this time she was having sex with a fucking ghost or whatever the fuck it is.

I stood in the street. The birds began to sing and I knew it was only an hour or so to sunrise. I was furious and frightened. You really have no idea what it is like. How would you react if you saw that? What would you do? Say it's *O.K* and put on the kettle? This had happened at my home too and she had lied about it.

I thought how fucking dare she stop having sex with me but have sex with that thing instead. That's how irrational I was at the time. You can't think clearly when something as horrendous as that happens and I was furious. It wasn't her fault; I witnessed that with my own eyes. She had no control over it. It was not as if she was consciously encouraged it; it was not as if she wanted it. It was not like she had been hiding texts from me, lying to me, meeting men behind my back, encouraging them to embark on an affair to satisfy her own selfish needs. I was hurt as like an affair she thought or hoped that I would never find out, that any suspicion she could simply hide behind a lie. This was different, Lisa didn't intend any hurt on me, she had tried to protect me by not telling me but I wish I had known. Maybe if I was prepared then maybe I could have helped her or found a way to help her.

She didn't tell me because she said she didn't want to lose me. I don't know if I would have done had she told me. Would I have believed her or simply tried to find a rational explanation to try and help her? What I witnessed has no rational explanation. It was a transgression. Lisa has been betrayed by God and by nature for this to happen. This should not happen by how our world works and no psychological condition or physical abnormality can be held responsible for this. This was a supernatural power, evil and disgusting, enjoying tearing the love from two people that had done nothing wrong.

Lisa: Daniel left me. He didn't return any of my calls for a few days and he wouldn't answer the door when I went to see him. He was hurt like no other. I rang him and he answered and I told him everything, I did not hide the truth or make any excuses. I told him everything. He was just quiet on the phone and he said he would call me soon. I spoke to him a few days later on the phone and he sobbed down the phone and told me he was sorry, sorry that he couldn't help me; sorry he couldn't love someone who had that happening to them. He was never the same. He was signed off on the sick for two months with depression. He left his job and he quietly disappeared from my life.

I'm not sure how long I cried for when he hung up after he finished with me. I had this huge empty feeling inside. It wasn't my fault and I loved him so much and the hurt, the hurt that man felt eats me up to this day. I know I can't stop what is happening to me but maybe I should have told him the truth or maybe I should never have gone out with him. I was selfish in that I wanted a normal life, a life of love and happiness. I should have been stronger and resigned myself to the fact that this would never go away and because of my selfishness I broke a man.

I convinced myself that it would be different this time with Daniel that something as good and pure as we had could beat anything, even ghosts and spirits. I used to pray that maybe the spirit would be a kind spirit and see I was in love and be happy for me. I don't think it works like that. I don't think they work on the same wavelengths as us.

I think of Daniel when we were together, he was kind and caring. How we would sit snuggled up watching a movie or sat there in the sun eating dinner he made, drinking wine. He never complained about anything, encouraged me in every aspect of my life and was so proud of me when we were with his friends. He made me feel young and alive and he made me feel loved. I guess when there is a wrong doing in a relationship and it's your own fault that you hope that the other person finds happiness, to remove that feeling of guilt and shame. Daniel will never find that happiness.

It has been two years since Dan left and it still happens, the assaults I mean. They happen here at home, but not as frequently as when Daniel was with me. It is like it thrived off the power of breaking Dan and me up. I went on holiday with Tyler and his girlfriend to Brighton a few months ago to a holiday cottage on the coast and it happened there too. I think that regardless of where I am or who I am with, it has me when it wants too. I can't help that my body reacts the way it does to it but emotionally and mentally I take no pleasure from it. I wonder will it stop when I am old and haggard or will it continue to my dying day. One thing I do know is that my fate is to be alone for the rest of my life. I will never feel the love and compassion of another man again.

Investigation

The testimonials from Lisa and Daniel on the events that led to their detachment are both tragic and disturbing. Clearly we have two individuals that shared an emotional connection only for it to be severed by the paranormal intrusion. Could a metaphysical being cause such alienation between the two or could there be a more rational explanation for the estrangement?

The encounters and descriptions of the events do have continuity and emotional countenance that led me to believe this is not a hoax. My role, my honour as an investigator, is to delve into every facet of the account and sift through the information to differentiate the fact from the fiction and hopefully discern a probable explanation.

During the interviews I believed that everyone involved had a sense of conviction and that the events bestowed upon them had abundantly affected them in a deep and profound way. I believed that something was happening to Lisa and was affecting those around her.

I was fortunate enough to be joined by, A.S Hawkings, a psychologist, for this investigation and she was able to give me some possible explanations into what was happening. Now A.S Hawkins can only make her hypothesis based on the information we have received and these are not definitive answers but more of a probable likelihood.

ASH: I would not wish to dispute Lisa's integrity; the events in her life have been extremely traumatic. I have spoken to her, with you, at length and she believes what is happening to her to be real. I have observed during these testimonials and she has displayed no micro expressions associated with deceit or misrepresentation. I would say that she strongly believes that what is happening has happened.

I have many theories and ideas on what may be behind the perception of what the family believes to be occurring. In fact a whole separate book could be written on this. What I have done is given a few succinct ideas on the causes behind the alleged events. I would say to your readers, that, these are not definitive answers and without continued investigation we will be unable to define the explanation. I think it is certainly food for thought for the readers.

Now, there is a condition known as Sleep sex, or Sexsomnia, it is a condition in which a person will engage in sexual activities while still asleep. This condition falls within the broad classes of sleep disorders known as parasomnia. In extreme cases, Sexsomnia has been alleged as the cause of rare instances of sexual assault, including rape.

Sexsomnia is considered a type of non-rapid eye movement sleep. Sexsomniacs do not remember the acts that they perform while they are asleep. Sexsomnia can co-occur alongside other sleep disorders such as sleepwalking, sleep apnea, night terrors and bedwetting and can be triggered by stress, previous sleep deprivation and excessive consumption of alcohol or drugs. Sleep related epilepsy may be associated with sexual arousal, pelvic thrusting and orgasms, though in these sorts of cases the acts are often not remembered. Sexsomnia episodes could be triggered by physical contact with a bed partner. It is a fairly new medically recognized behaviour, has been used in criminal defence cases of rape.

 Now this does not explain what Tyler or Daniel claimed to have witnessed. A broad hypothesis would be that they experienced a hallucination. Visual hallucinations involve seeing things that aren't there. The hallucinations may be of objects, visual patterns, people, and or lights. For example, you might see a person who is not in the room or flashing lights that no one else can see. This may explain the *electrical orbs* that were seen in the house.

Hallucinations are sensations that appear real but are created by your mind. They can affect all five of your senses. For example, you might hear a voice that no one else in the room can hear or see an image that is not real. These symptoms may be caused by mental illness, the side effects of medications, or physical illnesses like epilepsy or alcoholism. Treatment may include taking medication to cure a physical or mental illness or adopting healthier behaviours like drinking less alcohol and getting more sleep.

Hallucinations are false or distorted sensory experiences that seem real and may be seen, heard, felt, and even smelled or tasted, yet are generated only by the mind. A hallucination occurs when a misfire occurs within the mechanism of the brain that helps to distinguish conscious perceptions from internal, memory-based perceptions.

I have known of a case where a woman claimed to hear people in her home and this was always at the time of her period. She was diagnosed with PMMD, the most severe form of premenstrual syndrome which was affecting her hormonal and brain wave activity and was creating very real hallucinations. A course of medication soon eradicated the symptoms and the voices ceased to exist.

Sleep states and altered states of consciousness can lead people to believe that they have experienced something supernatural. For example, sceptics have used sleep paralysis or a hypnogogic trance to explain encounters in which people see spirits while in bed and are unable to move or escape. Most people experience a hypnogogic trance once or twice in their lives, although it is far more common in people with epilepsy or certain sleep disorders.

In regards to the sense of people in the house or even shadowy figures being seen in the home there is research to explain what may be happening. When Swiss scientists electrically stimulated an epileptic patient's brain, the patient, reported a shadow person sitting behind her copying her every move. When she sat up, it also sat up. When she bent forward and grabbed her knees, it reached around her body and held her. The doctors then told her to read a card, but the shadow person tried to take it out of her hand. The scientists had stimulated the left temporoparietal junction, the part of the brain that defines the idea of self. By interfering with the area that helps us tell the difference between ourselves and others, the doctors confused the brain's ability to understand its own body, thus leading to the creation of a copycat shadow person. Researchers are hoping this is the key to understanding why so many people, both schizophrenic and healthy, encounter shadow beings and other creatures like aliens. Tyler claimed that there were electrical charges, like a static in the home before and during the paranormal experiences. It is possible that somehow an unknown electrical discharge was affecting the activity of their brains and causing these perceived events to be seen as real.

I sound exceptionally sceptical to the events that Lisa and her family have endured but I do believe that there are rational explanations for some of these metaphysical activities. My concern is for Lisa. I have offered to refer her to a general practitioner and a counsellor to help her make sense of what has happened, to ensure she has the full support of professionals that can work towards a solution. It is in everybody's best interest that Lisa is allowed to live a normal life.

***

I was granted a full week to fully investigate Lisa's home. I would have the house for two days to runs tests and evaluate the house to remove any natural causes and then a further four days with Lisa in the home.

I was mindful of the hypotheses generated by A.S Hawkings and included them into my investigation. I had to be sure that what was happening to Lisa was a physiological condition.

Lisa had taken her leave, along with Tyler and I had her home for a few days. The house has no untoward countenance on entry. There is no feeling of doom or a brooding presence. It is for all intents and purposes an ordinary, home in an ordinary street. I had spent many a long hour investigating the history of the home. The house had been built in the late nineteen fifties and had been built on farmland. I studied the census in detail and

I could not find any history of any building or structure built on the land.

Lisa was the third person to live in the home. The previous occupants were an old couple that lived there until nineteen seventy nine and then an elderly lady then lived alone in the house until her death a few months before Lisa and Tyler moved in. The lady that had lived there had died peacefully at Withybush Hospital and not in the home.

My next step was to conceive and establish a family tree for Lisa's family. I was hoping that within the family tree that I may discover a history of seemingly related medical or psychological conditions or even those that had participated in arcane practices. Alas my search proved inconclusive.

I have to have a balance during an investigation but I was still mindful of the possibility of an Incubus. An Incubus is a demon in male form that, according to a number of mythological and legendary traditions, lies upon sleepers, especially women, in order to have sexual intercourse with them. Its female counterpart is the succubus. An incubus may pursue sexual relations with a woman in order to father a child. Religious tradition holds that repeated intercourse with an incubus or succubus may result in the deterioration of health, or even death. I have had dealings with those that have allegedly had intercourse with such entities. I have included these for your perusal at the end of this account.

The first thing that any good paranormal investigator should do is examine the place of the haunting with thorough detail. You need to establish where every cold spot is, what noises the house makes and what factors may influence a rational mind into believing that something paranormal is happening. With the aid of a thermal imaging device I was able to determine where there were natural cold and warm spots in the home. A thermal camera, also called an infrared camera or thermal imaging camera is a device that forms an image using infrared radiation, similar to a common camera that forms an image using visible light. This also gave me accurate temperature readings. I found a cold spot on the landing that was streaming in from the attic hatchway and once up there I found a missing tile on the roof. Could this be responsible for the cold spots encountered? Lisa, Tyler and Daniel all complained about freezing temperatures on the landing. I would keep evaluating the temperatures on the landing and see to which level they would drop to,

The house of course had settling noises and the neighbours next door might have been non-existent for the amount of noise they made. With Night vision cameras, thermal imaging, digital audio recorders, motion sensors and web cams set up in every room, I settled in for my first night. Alone, I made myself comfortable in Lisa's bedroom.

I lay on Lisa's bed, alone, and contemplated the disturbing events that had taken place in this house, in this room and in this very bed. I did not feel malice or rancour but a feeling of melancholy for Lisa. Regardless if this was a psychological condition or a genuine paranormal materialization surely everyone is entitled to have a normal and loving relationship? Surely this woman is entitled to sleep at peace in the night without the fear and trauma of inexplicable violations. What sort of hurt must Lisa feel to lose not only Dan, but Leon and Ian? For no fault of her own she has endured a horrific experience that we can only begin to contemplate through the safety of written words in a book or magazine or through a Hollywood movie.

Over the first two days I stayed there, I experienced no unusual activity. The temperature on the landing remained around the same constant temperature.

I was met on the third day by a female paranormal investigator who would be monitoring Lisa and her sleep patterns. I would remain vigilant at the bank of monitors and readouts in the living room. From there I had full scope of the house. If anything were to happen to Lisa, I would be there.

For four nights we were sat there and for those four nights nothing happened. I know it must be a tremendous disappointment to you, the reader, but we cannot fabricate fictitious findings. I cannot in good faith sensationalize a traumatic and confounding series of events just for the purpose of entertainment. Like, yourself, we were most disappointed. However the person most upset was Lisa. She really hoped that we would find something or witness something that would help her make sense of what had happened to her and those close to her. We of course have thousands of hours of video footage and audio to sift through and a thorough examination of these is time consuming and we hope that somewhere hidden in a split second of footage is a clue to the events of that home.

Lisa was concerned that lack of evidence would deem her a fraudster. I reassured her that the investigation was not to prove she had manipulated and deceived but that we had hoped to find some solid and conclusive evidence that would help her come to terms with her experiences.

We are welcome back to the home and we shall conduct further investigations but we have discovered nothing. Metaphysical activities cannot be conjured up at a whim. They cannot be controlled or cajoled into existence. If such things were to exist then they will manifest at a time and place befitting their own uncanny needs. Who knows what really happened to Lisa in this home. What had broken Daniel to become a shadow of his former self? What was behind the haunting activities? And was Lisa a victim of a long term and abusive sexual violation? I shall continue my investigation and one day hope to have the answers that Lisa, richly, deserves.

This is not the end. There are a few more answers that I need to add to the comprehensive research on this case. There may be more to this than meets the eye. There are two people in particular that have more to add to this story.

Onan

I had the sense that Tyler had begun to warm to me over the last several weeks. He had opened up and displayed genuine emotion in regards to the events surrounding his mother. We have to realize that if this account is true then Tyler has witnessed things that no child should of their parent. Despite the rapport we had, I knew that Tyler was hiding something from me. I had to establish if this was something vital to the case. I sat down with him for our final interview session and I was absolute in my determination to bring this missing piece of the puzzle into the light. Tyler was stubborn and strong-willed but He knew that the full account had to be told and eventually he acquiesced. This is Tyler final words on the terrifying events that took place in the home.

Tyler: I never wanted to talk about this. I never wanted to talk about any of this. If people think it happened to Mum, then they might think it was happening to me. People might think I'm gay or something. I don't want people thinking that I was having sex with a ghost or some shit. Nothing like that happened but there was one day when something really strange happened. I didn't want to tell you. This is Mum's ordeal and her story and this is just embarrassing. I would burn him if I could, I would destroy him for what it did to us.

I was around eighteen; I was in my room, my old room. Mum was out one afternoon at work. I was lying in bed reading a magazine. It was a porno mag O.K? I had picked it up at a newsagent in Haverfordwest as I didn't want anyone to see me buying it here in the Dock. It was only *Readers wives*, you know, the one with the Milfs? Well you know what you're like when you're eighteen? I was enjoying the magazine so to speak. I was...masturbating. There's nothing wrong with that. I'm doing it in my own home. Mum is out. It's not like I'm a pervert. Most men I know crank one out to pornography.

I'm reading away when there is this overpowering smell of shit in the room. The same awful smell that would herald the arrival of the shitty man. I stop and next thing something really hard hits me in the face. Full on hits me. It hit me with enough force to knock me down onto the pillow and it left a red mark. I'm shocked as fuck and then the magazine just launches across the room. The magazine by its own flew across the room and fluttered against the wall and fell on the floor in a heap. I was too shocked to yell. I was shaking like a shitting dog.

Then the smell disappeared and it was as if nothing had happened at all. If it was not for the stinging on my face it could have been that I had dreamt it. I was furious. I wanted to smash something up. It was so humiliating and I was powerless to retaliate. I'm lying there with my dick out and with a hand mark across my face.

Obviously it makes you weary to do anything like that again or bring girls back home but thankfully it only happened once, well to me, we know what happened to Mum. I think it was sending me a message. I can't think why it would hit me and what it had against my porno mag. No one will know what the motives of that stinking fuck the shitty man will ever be. He's not been back since and I pray he never does. If I could then I would ruin him. I would torture him for a lifetime for what he did to us. I hate him so much. If your house ever starts to stink that bad and you can't find a cause then just get out of there. It might be the shitty man and you cannot stop him.

Revelation

There was another person I felt had something to add to this. Judith. She claimed to have had knowledge passed to her from the spirit realm on the identity of one of the spirits in the home. Could it be true? If so could this person be investigated and linked to the home? Maybe there was one final possibility to solve this and perhaps we could help a spirit find peace and leave our plain of existence. Was this spirit the one responsible for the attacks on Lisa? Was it the disgustingly christened *Shitty man* or the one dubbed the *Cold man*?

Judith despite being ostracized by her family for her involvement in the events was more than willing to shed some light on the perpetrator. She hoped that by revealing his identity that Lisa may reach out and reconcile with her and bring her back into the family.

Judith: I understand why Lisa is so angry with me. I really do. When we cleansed the house there were two spirits there. There was one that was evil and dank and another that just wanted to be close to her. The spirit world had changed and confused it so much it was as if it had two minds. Maybe he had mental health issues in life. This is how confused the spirit is. It is like it is fighting with itself sometimes but at its core the intention is nothing but good.

I ask you now that if you had the power to stop a family from breaking apart then would you? If you could keep everyone in that family together then I would hope that you would make that right choice. Lisa cannot understand but I made a choice for her and Tyler. I sacrificed being part of this family for them and they don't realize it. Every family has the right to be together.

Rose was the first to tell me that he was dead and I was surprised. I didn't know he had died. I did not know he had passed. When I came to the house I felt the presence of the evil and filthy one but there was another force there battling with it. I sensed it was him and when I did my research and found out he had been killed then everything started to make sense. I can show you the newspaper clippings. Lisa never knew, Lisa was never told. Lisa believed he simply vanished. Lisa believed that he no longer loved her but he did. He never stopped loving her and he wanted to come back to her but he wasn't allowed. Once he had died then there was nothing stopping him. He is never far from Lisa; he is never far from Tyler. He is their Guardian Angle.

Every child deserves to be close to their Dad and that is what I Did. I allowed Ian to remain close to Lisa and Tyler and it is Ian that is protecting them. Ian's love for Lisa never died. He never wanted to leave and now the three of them are together. Ian's parents tore his world apart and now he is back and they cannot interfere this time. Ian just wants to be close to his son and be with his sweetheart.

I don't want you to tell Lisa. I want her to find out for herself. When she reads this then she will know the pain and sacrifice I have been through for her. I may not have Lisa but I still have my Rose.

I may have to wait until we are all passed to be part of the family again but until then I am happy knowing that I did the right thing for my child and my grandson. One day Rose, Lisa, Tyler, Ian and I will be together and we shall walk in fields under the sun. I look forward to that time.

Epilogue

I am puzzled by so much that has happened to this family. Is it simply a cacophony of psychological conditions that has affected the people in the home? Have the family created an elaborate fiction for motives unknown only to themselves? Dare we believe that metaphysical bodies are entering our realm to abuse and violate us? Has a long lost love truly returned to his family? Despite Judith's assurances of evidence I could find none relating to Ian.

As is always a danger of prolonged exposure to the witness's and I have grown fond of Lisa. I admire her courage and determination. This is a woman that always put her son first. This is a woman like so many of you reading this had so many hopes and dreams of a normal life. She wants to love and be loved and the environment surrounding her makes this almost impossible.

Through the many weeks that the interviews took place, I always questioned her motives for doing this and the answer was always the same: *I want to help others that maybe going through this.*

She hopes that no one ever has to suffer in the fashion that she has but she knows that she is not alone that there are others like her out there. Despite the continuing threat of violation she is tenacious. She continues to work and support her adult son and she always finds something good in the day to comment on. This is a woman resigned to her fate. This is a woman that has sacrificed the love of a good man to protect them. This is a woman destined to be alone forever.

Further research will continue and any findings will be posted on the paranormalchronicles.com website and before we have Lisa's final words I ask you one last time. What would you do if this was happening to you?

Lisa: Some days I feel lonely. I feel sad inside. You take for granted a hug or the touch of a hand. To lie next to someone, held in their arms, would be just as nice as a full night of passion. This will never happen again. I cannot allow anyone into my life again. You saw what it did to Daniel.

I see people walking hand in hand in the street or customers where I work and I smile. I feel so happy for them and I hope they appreciate it. I see people arguing and I just wish they would stop and realize how lucky they are to be together.

I think about those perfect times with Leon or Dan. Those days when you wake up and they are lying next to you, asleep. I would look at them, so peaceful and I would slowly lift my hand to just stroke their face. Little things like that are the things you miss the most.

I put a brave face on but sometimes the loneliness hurts so much. A girl I work with is always down on her boyfriend. He cooks and rubs her feet and he does nice things for her all the time but she doesn't know what she wants and you can see it in his eyes when he comes to pick her up from work that he adores her. He thinks so much of her and yet she is so blind to how this man would never want to hurt her, cheat on her or put her down. She is blind to that this one man would do anything for her but all she thinks and talks about is other men. I would do anything in the world just to have that feeling of being wanted again. I want to be part of something so amazing. I want someone to be there for me when I finish my shift with a hug and a cup of tea. I will never have the bath run for me or breakfast made for me in a romantic way. I will never stand in a card shop picking out a Valentines card or snuggled up watching a movie or making up after an argument. I lie in bed some nights just wishing that someone would text me goodnight to say they love me. It's nice just to know that there is someone out there thinking of you. These are such simple things that people take for granted. I want to feel loved.

When I was sixteen I'd imagine getting married and having children. I imagined buying a house and having a garden and having friends and family over. I thought I would be nurse or a policewoman. It's strange how things work out. I have Tyler and he is my world. He is a man now and it will only be a matter of time that that he leaves for good to have the life he wants.

I wish Tyler had never had to see the things he had to. I wish none of this had ever happened but every day when I get up I just thank God that I have Tyler. I would not change a thing. He is my life.

The attacks are frequent now. Maybe six or seven times a year. I lie there and let it carry on. I don't fight them or cry afterwards. Once it is done I just go to sleep. It never hurts me and since I have had no boyfriends come to the house it hasn't done anything but have sex with me.

I've tried to just like it, enjoy it, but it is too strange and unnatural to just accept. I don't have any sexual pleasure in my life at all. I don't pleasure myself. What it does has ruined that part of my life. I see what it does the same as having a migraine. It's there and I just wait until it has passed. One night it lasted for hours and another night a few minutes. I guess the spirits are just like men in our world in that respect then.

I don't know what it sees in me. I don't know what its fixation is with me and I often wonder if one day it will ever stop. I wonder how I will feel the day it finally ends? Maybe by then I will have come to accept it and I will be sad. I will never have peace as I will always wonder when it will come back.

I am glad the Cold man beat the shitty man as I could not endure its abuse any longer. If that had carried on then I have no doubts that I would have taken my own life. It is strange to think that I have become acceptant of a lesser of two evils.

I think about Daniel a lot. He was a good man. He did nothing wrong but love me. I have never known someone so supportive of my life. He encouraged me to do the things that made me happy. He believed that if you were happy inside that you would make others happy. Now he's miserable and alone and it's all because of me.

If someone reads this and they think I'm insane then think what you will. I am happy for you to be able to think like that as that means that this has not happened to you. There are others out there that have been assaulted and abused by these paranormal rapists. I have read about them online and in books. I didn't want it in my life and I wish I could be the one reading this book and thinking *poor cow* or *bullshit*.

I want nothing but for my story to be told and for people out there to realize that there are strange and terrible things that pass into our world. I want people to hold on to what they love so much. Fight for the things you care for the most and to enjoy every second of every day. I want people reading this to tell the people in their lives that they love them, to hug them, to appreciate them.

For if what happened to me happens to you then you can kiss all of that goodbye.

Supplementary

The account as told by Lisa and her family is not a unique encounter. Even in this small part of the world which I inhabit, has had its fair share of paranormal sexual activity.

These are just raw accounts as presented by those that claim to have had encounters of a sexual kind in Pembrokeshire and no investigations have taken place into their validity at this time. Two of these transgressions have been published at www.theparanormalchronicles.com and the third and final report is brand new and exclusive to this novel.

Like the investigation that you have just embarked on these accounts are sexually detailed and explicit and may cause offense. Each one is from a very different perspective in terms of the demographic that the witness represents.

We ask that you read and then digest the information and theorise on the plausibility of such things. In the world of the paranormal there is no right or wrong as of yet as no one has had conclusive and sustainable evidence that can be presented to the people of the world. We have our own experience and our own opinions of course and we are always delighted to hear yours. Whether you are a sceptic or a believer your opinions matters to those at the paranormal chronicles so please get in touch and we can discuss it further.

Lisa's tale maybe over for now but the ghost sex phenomenon continues as you are about to experience. We hope that if you are reading this that it has not or will not happen to you.

Succubus

From all over the world we have received messages from those that believe that they have been subjected to a paranormal sexual encounter (54% of voters on a paranormal chronicles poll believe a ghost can have sex with a person) and of course the backlash from those that we unintentionally offended who were appalled at the notion that such a thing could take place or that ghosts exist. Again it is for you the reader to decide based on your own philosophies and beliefs to determine what actually occurred to this man from Milford Haven in Pembrokeshire.

We of course are not here to offend, we are here to report on the Paranormal and let you the readers dissect the information and question and validate on the merits and idea's presented in the accounts in your own personal fashion. We always give warning that the material may be inappropriate and that due caution be taken before you delve into the report. Never have those words rung as true as we prepare to take you on a most disturbing and unsettling account of a man's ghost sex experience on a roadside in Pembrokeshire.

We ask that if you are easily offended to perhaps explore one of our other blogs such as the truly horrific stinking men encounter or the baffling owl man mystery as for this account that we present is of a graphic and explicit nature that will make you think twice before you pick up a stranger on the road again.

John contacted us a few days after we published the original ghost sex blog on our Facebook page. He said that he was local, from Milford Haven and that he had, had a most awful and dumbfounding experience on a roadside in Pembrokeshire a few months ago. We relayed several messages back and forth until he agreed that we could telephone him and conduct an interview to publish on the Paranormal Chronicles. Like so many that allow us to publish their accounts they hope that others like them have had the same or similar experience and may help them make sense of what happened. John is a man in his mid-twenties and this is his account in his own words. Once again we appeal to your rationale that if you are easily offended then to please stop reading this now as not only does it contain a disturbing and frightening paranormal experience but has sexually explicit language that some may feel is inappropriate.

John: I was driving back from Swansea one afternoon around 4ish. I had met a woman online and I went up on the Friday to meet her and see how we got on. She was nice enough but she looked nothing like she did on her dating profile; her pic must have been from years ago before she had kids. Anyway I was on my way home, I had radio 1 on and I wasn't looking forward to going back to work the following day. I was tired as I had been up late and I spent the day with this woman in Swansea having food, going to the cinema and stuff.

I was on the A40 road between St Clears and Whitland when it started to rain; it was starting to get dark too when I noticed up ahead a woman with her thumb out. As I got closer I realised that she was well fit and I thought I would give her a lift as she was probably not going too far so if she was a nutter then I wouldn't have to be with her for long. I slowed down and saw that she was in a short black dress, black high heels and a small handbag. I thought either she was coming home from a night out or was on her way out. There were no other cars on the road so I slowed down and pulled in a few feet from where she was. The rain had started to come down quite hard but she took for ever to get in, *I kept thinking you silly cow do you want a lift or not?*

She eventually got in, her black hair matted to her face. She must have been freezing. I said hello and she looked over at me and pushed her hair from her face and she was stunning, so beautiful, she must have been the same age as me maybe a bit younger. She sat in and put her seatbelt on and *said "Thank you so much."* I asked where was she going and she replied *"Haverfordwest."* I asked her how she was out here all alone and she said her boyfriend had a row and he had kicked her out in the middle of nowhere. I said he was a prick to do that and that I would get her to Haverfordwest. She smiled and asked first that I wasn't a serial killer or anything and I laughed and said not today. I drove off and a song came up on the radio and she turned it up and she said she loved this song. We drove listening to the song and she turned the radio down and asked where had I been and I explained about the online dating and she laughed when I said that the woman wasn't exactly what I had been hoping for but then she said *"I bet you still shagged her though"* and we both laughed. I kept looking at her pale legs as her short black dress was hitched up on her thighs. She caught me looking and she smiled at me and I pretended like nothing had happened. As we were getting close to Narberth she said that there was a roadside rest stop and could we pop in there for a moment as she said the toilets there might be open and she was desperate to go. I pulled in and the rain was hammering on the car and as soon as I stopped she undid her seatbelt and started to kiss me. I didn't say no and let her carry on. Before I knew it she had undid my jeans and got my penis out and just started sucking it. It was incredible, so horny, like some story out of a porno mag. You never think anything like this can happen to you. I thought I was going to cum but she stopped, pulled her dress up, pulled her black panties to one side and got on top of me and slid down on top of my stiffy. It was fantastic. She pushed my head into her chest and up and down she went.

Then I started to smell something strange, at first I thought it was like a cigarette smell but then I noticed that it was like burning plastic. The woman shoved her tongue in my mouth and it tasted like shit, actual shit but she wouldn't take her tongue from out my mouth. I thought I was going to be sick. Then it felt like my penis was being scraped by sandpaper or grit, the pain was horrendous. I tried to push her off but it felt like her tongue was going further down my throat, I was choking, and I thought I was going to die. I was crying and everything. I was passing out. I just wanted a police man or a dogger to start banging on the window and save me.

I pushed her back with all my force and there was not a pretty girl on me but some haggard, disgusting old woman with some kind of awful skin condition. I just screamed and screamed and somehow I came and she just vanished. I swear she just vanished and I was sat there on my own with my cock out.

I picked up a fit woman and got raped by an old haggard thing. I had not been drinking and I don't do drugs. I got out of the car in the rain, it was near dark and there was no one there. I searched the back seat, the boot everywhere. I even looked under the bonnet. I was scared to get back in but I did and I got home. I cried for every second it took to get home. I live alone and I was terrified. The next day I got my car checked at the garage as I thought maybe it was the exhaust, you know the fumes, carbon monoxide poisoning but there was nothing wrong with my car.

What the fuck was that thing and why me? I will never ever pick up anyone again and I have driven that road a million times since hoping to see that woman again so I can call the police and get her arrested. I have no idea what happened but I still have nightmares about it now.

***

As an investigator it is always difficult to try and evaluate the events that occur without actually being there or witnessing them yourself. Was this merely an illusion, maybe the man's disappointment at his date manifested into a waking day dream of picking up a beautiful and sexual promiscuous woman was suddenly changed into a nightmare fuelled by guilt and shame? Was this perhaps a Succubus? A female demon or supernatural entity in folklore (traced back to medieval legend) that appears in dreams and takes the form of a human woman in order to seduce men, usually through sexual activity. (The male counterpart is the incubus. Religious traditions hold that repeated sexual activity with a succubus may result in the deterioration of health or even death)

Was this creature merely in an appealing guise to entrap this man and take his seed? If so then what agenda does it have for the man's genetic soup? What profane and insidious plan has it for a human child born of a demon? If such things were to exist...

Whatever was behind this terrifying and horrific event I think we should all learn the lesson of not to pick up hitch-hikers, especially on the stretch of road between St Clears and Whitland.

Mary

We love your emails and messages that we receive at the Paranormal Chronicle offices and your feedback, opinions and stories inspire us on our journey into the unknown. You may have gathered that We like to pose questions and dilemma's to you and we hope that when you read our investigations, our accounts and our e-novels and that you ponder and ask yourself *"what would I have done?"* We certainly hope that you ask yourself that question after reading this heart breaking account.

This tragic account is from a lady from Fishguard, Pembrokeshire who was unfortunate enough to have an experience with an extremely sexually promiscuous female spirit that turned her attention to her husband...on their honeymoon.

Here in her own words is the account that Samantha experienced during her honeymoon.

Samantha: The wedding day was perfect. You could not have asked for a better day. We had married in a small old church on the coast and travelled up to Fishguard to have the reception. I had met Dave a year before online and he had moved down to Pembrokeshire and he had popped the question.

We were very much in love and we were at an age where it was good to meet someone and settle down. I was in my mid-forties and Dave was in his early fifties. Neither of us had children but it was nice to think that we would have each other and companionship till our dying day.

We had our friends and family down and it was a beautiful day, I didn't need a lavish dress or a Rolls Royce to pick me up it was all about being together and being with our friends and family. We were blessed with sunshine, the smell of the sea and great people.

We had decided that we would book into a coastal hotel up in Cardiganshire. We had been to Spain and Malta in the year so we didn't need anything fancy or expensive just a nice quiet place where we could be together. We wanted somewhere quiet and romantic.

We got to the hotel and it was lovely, quaint and old fashioned and you could see the coast from the car park, it was lovely. We went into reception and there were all these old photos from the 19th century. There was an old man at the reception with a bald head and big white pork chop whiskers and he was very polite and helpful and as he carried our bags to the honeymoon suite. He said that some of the guests had complained about Red Mary, a broken hearted ghost, who had lost her husband at sea and had slept around to feel accepted. A newlywed couple had found her dead in the bathroom of the hotel with her wrists slashed. It seemed that no other woman could have a man but her and she went out of her way to cause marital problems and eventually her despair consumed her and committed the act of suicide. Dave and I laughed and joked as we don't believe in that kind of thing.

That night, I put on my sexy nightwear ready to consummate the marriage, not that we had saved ourselves, not at all, but tradition is good. Dave was in the bathroom for ages and I thought, *I hope he is ok* and I opened the door and he was stood there naked, eyes closed, with an erection. I asked him if he was *O.K.* and he looked startled and shocked and quickly grabbed a towel and covered himself up. He was red in the face and he was looking around the bathroom all confused. I thought maybe he was just knocking one out so he would perform better. I am no prude and masturbation is a key part of sexual activity as far as I am concerned.

I grabbed him by the arm and led him to bed and I began to pleasure his tumescence but he seemed distant and showed no interest. He lost his rigidity and asked that he be excused to go to the bathroom. I was curious to why he was so prudish as we had been very wild and adventurous over the last year.

I lay there and Dave was gone another five minutes or so and I got up and I went back into the bathroom and there he was again. Naked, proud as a trooper, eyes closed, holding his hand just above his crotch area like he was rubbing something. I was furious. I asked him what he thought he was doing and he panicked again and said *"Nothing, nothing, just getting ready."* And he had the audacity to ask for another five minutes peace!!

I was livid and I put on my coat and stormed out of the room and headed to the bar. I sat there with a gin and tonic expecting him to come down and apologise. He didn't and I could understand what had gotten into him. It's an awful shock to think that maybe you have married the wrong man that might have some issues. Twenty minutes passed and I though damn him and I stormed up and barged into the room and the sick bastard was sat in bed, again with an erection and was making weird sucking noise with his mouth. He was flicking his tongue in and out and his hands were moving as if on an invisible body. I was shocked and then I watched him ejaculate in a huge squirt even though there was nothing stimulating his penis. I screamed at him and he jumped off the bed and said that it was all her fault. I screamed at him who was he referring to and he said the woman and was pointing frantically into the corner of the room. I could see no one but my perverted new husband standing naked and shamed.

I did what any sane woman should do and that was to throw him out. He protested and was adamant that she was in there. I was furious. I had married a lunatic and now it was all over. Everything had been for nothing.

I lay on the bed sobbing and I sat up and for a quick second through my blurry eye I saw a naked woman, in her early thirties with long red hair flowing onto her chest. I was shocked and I saw the gaping gash's on her wrists where severe cuts had been made. She smiled a sickly smile and she simply vanished.

Had Dave been telling the truth? I spoke to him in the morning and I asked him to describe this woman and he said she had long red hair and pale skin. I was appalled. He said that it was like he was under a spell and he was addicted to her. I contacted the hotel owner the following week and asked more about the story and they said that a pale, red headed woman had been seen and either the husband or the wife staying there fled the room, but never both.

I tried to fix it with Dave but every time I saw him or he attempted to touch me I saw his face, his shame from that night and after four months we were over and he moved back to Brighton.

Years later I was re-searching the haunting and found out that the room was no longer a honeymoon suite and a fire had gutted that side of the hotel and the remains of the room had been made into two single rooms, not doubt concealing a tremendous surprise for lonely travelling businessmen.

I never believed till that night in ghosts but a spirit defiantly broke my marriage and I say to any honeymooners that you check the room you are staying in first. If that room has history of the supernatural then don't risk it. Find another hotel!!

Forever

It would be easy to believe that the inhabitants of the supernatural realm have little regard for our own well-being. We are submissive to a powerful force then undertakes a range of debase and degrading sexual and physical acts upon us. However there is one such account that I wish to leave you with. It is the testimonial from a charming lady in her eighties. It is a story of hope, faith and love and I do hope that this sends you away from this book with a less depressing demeanour.

I met with Jean at her home several miles from Solva in Western Pembrokeshire. Jean is a kindly lady with a wicked sense of humour. She sits me down and proudly shows me the pictures of her three children, eight grandchildren and two great grandchildren that adorn her living room dresser.

One picture she picks up and hands to me. It is a black and white picture of a couple on their wedding day.

Jean: This is me and George on our wedding day. It was raining but it didn't matter. I wanted to marry George from the first day I set eyes on him. What a handsome man. We married in 1947. George was back from the army and we got a small cottage up by the farm where he got work. Harold, our first son, was born on Halloween of all days and two years later on February 13th Michael was born. George wanted a daughter so much and on March 30th 1955, Louise was born, and he was so thrilled. He loved his children so much. We were all so happy. I look back then and it was prefect. They say good things don't last.

George was killed in a tractor accident two weeks after Louise was born. It was heart-breaking. I was so angry with God that he took the man I loved away from me. I had three beautiful children to raise and no husband and they would have no father.

Years went by and one night I woke up and George was on top of me. He was being intimate. I was so shocked. I thought it was a dream. It was a very pleasurable dream. Then it happened again and again. He never says anything when he has relations with me. In fact he says nothing at all. Years went by and he never aged.

I'm 87 years old and George still makes love to me. I have never had to find another man and I love him just the same as when he was alive. I wish sometimes that he could do other things like fix the cupboard or get some shopping in though.

It was queer at first as he never said a word. At first I was frightened but then I realized that it was just George. I could feel him and once it was over he would simply vanish. I made a joke to him once about phantom pregnancies but he just stared at me in silence and kept rutting away.

George still comes to me even though I am an old woman. It makes me happy to think that he sneaks off from heaven just to see his old lady. He loves me for who I am not who I was. I know that when it's my turn to pass on that he will be there waiting for me and when we are together again we will both be young as we were. If you love someone that much and so strongly then that love will never die and every day I think once I get to heaven we can start all over again but this time we will never be apart.

About the Author

Pembrokeshire born G.L.Davies has been investigating the paranormal for over 25 years since he was 11. Despite issues with dyslexia he has completed a degree module on Hauntings in 19th century literature and is the founder of the www.theparanormalchronicles.com. His debut novel A Most Haunted house was an international bestseller. He has also conduced live investigations for 102.5 Radio Pembrokeshire and his paranormal reports have made national and international headlines. His objectivity and thorough investigative and interview techniques has made him one of Pembrokeshire's leading and respected paranormal investigators.

The Paranormal Chronicles

For further information for upcoming title releases, news and investigation updates then please visit:
www.theparanormalchronicles.com

You can also keep up to date with the paranormal chronicles future releases through twitter @paranormalchron and on Facebook at: www.facebook.com/theparanormalchronicles

The author would like to note that the Paranormal is a very sensitive subject and has appreciated your commitment to reading this novel. If you would like to contact him regarding anything that has been written about in this novel or for general information then please do so by emailing: paranormalchronicles@aim.com and will always appreciate any feedback, views, opinions, theories, beliefs and philosophies in a respectful and understanding manner.

Please feel free to recommend to a friend that enjoys the subject of the Paranormal. Please take the time to review this kindle title on Amazon. Your reviews are important.

Thank you.

Edited by R. L Armstrong. Without whom this book would never have been completed. Thank you

© Ghost sex: The Violation by G L Davies 2014

Read on for more from the Paranormal Chronicles.

A most haunted House

By G L Davies

Amazon #1 Bestseller in both Supernatural and Unexplained mystery categories in the U.K, U.S, Canada, Australia and Germany

A most haunted house is the worldwide bestseller based on a true and terrifying account of a prolific and aggressive haunting in a small Welsh town in West Wales. Seen as controversial and sparking debate between sceptics and believers alike due to the ferocity and intensity of the haunting, a most haunted house is the grim eye witness account of a young couple fighting to keep their new home and each other as an entity tears their world apart.

After an introduction by Investigator and paranormal re-searcher G L Davies, A most haunted house is a series of transcripts from the people involved that spans the three months that the haunting took place. Starting with almost small and mundane incidents and climaxing with the haunting reaching its full and terrifying ferocity.

Described as chilling and disturbing by some and thought provoking by others this is one novel that is a must for those interested in the Paranormal.

A most haunted house invites you the reader to decide for yourself on what truly happened at this home.

Should this be true, then there are unknown forces that we cannot combat in this world.

A most haunted house has been #1 in both the unexplained mystery and Supernatural categories on Kindle and has topped the charts since its release. Read today and join, as thousands already have, a journey into fear and the unknown.

What will you discover at A MOST HAUNTED HOUSE?

Reviews for a most haunted house

I have to say that this true story of a couple that are haunted by someone or something keeps you on your toes. Once I read the first page I was hooked and had to finish the book in one night. I must say that reading this alone in bed does make you feel is anyone watching you? This has to be one of the best paranormal books I've read, and I believe to be a true account of a couple's sad ghostly nightmare.

I loved this book from the start. Really felt for the couple that went through it, would recommend it to everyone.

I found this quite a gripping story all the more credible by the people concerned wanting no publicity. I could not put down the book until I had finished it.

Although it was a brilliant read I really started to feel some compassion for the couple. It was really chilling to know that something so powerful and not living could create so much devastation. I would definitely recommend.

A most compelling and chilling account for sceptics and believers alike of the unfortunate occurrences for a young couple in their first house. An emotional account of what should've been blissful beginnings but turned into a nightmare. A well recommended read!

What a well gripping story, a must for all supernatural fans. Buy yours today, a sure fire best seller!!!Waiting with baited breath for book No. 2

Very chilling and not to be read before going to bed! You are left to make your own judgement as to whether or not the story is real but it was very convincing

I love the style this book is written in, it gives it a raw edge and realism, like you are in the room with the author, listening with him as the victims recount their experiences I read in the reviews many times that the book was un-putdown able, and it truly is...I intended to spin it out and make it last a few evenings, but have read it in a couple of hours! I am so sorry for the couple, especially John. The way he repeats his concerns and advice for others who may be experiencing similar things is truly touching, and it is obvious that the effects of the house are far reaching, and still affecting him 10 years later. Personally I think this is a true account of a nightmarish experience, but even if it were a spoof I want to congratulate the author, it is superbly written and I would recommend it highly

Read it today on Kindle and Kindle app

Visit www.theparanormalchronicles.com for more paranormal investigations

Made in the USA
Middletown, DE
17 December 2019